I0474494

Improving Time
to
Profit

Improving Time to Profit

Customer Focused Strategies for Marketing and Sales

Meta-models and Best Practices

Kobi James

Writers Advantage

New York   Lincoln   Shanghai

Improving Time to Profit
Customer Focused Strategies for Marketing and Sales

All Rights Reserved © 2002 by Kobi James

No part of this book may be reproduced or transmitted in any form or by any means, graphic, electronic, or mechanical, including photocopying, recording, taping, or by any information storage retrieval system, without the permission in writing from the publisher.

Writers Advantage
an imprint of iUniverse, Inc.

For information address:
iUniverse
2021 Pine Lake Road, Suite 100
Lincoln, NE 68512
www.iuniverse.com

While there is no one magic bullet that will increase profitability, there are six bullets that will enable success.

ISBN: 0-595-24410-6

Printed in the United States of America

To those who identify the markets

and generate the revenue.

Contents

Introduction

"The real payoff for modern managers comes when they pounce on a great idea in one part of their empire and leverage it around the world."

—*Business Week/* 28 August 2000, p. 114

In the eighties, the push was for quality. Market share along with time to market was the focus of the nineties. The next thrust will be for profitability and the time it takes to get to profit. As shown in the diagram, the Time to Profit is the time that it takes for the profit stream of Area B to equal the sunk costs of Area A. This is in simplified terms, but Einstein once said we should never make things more complicated than they really are.

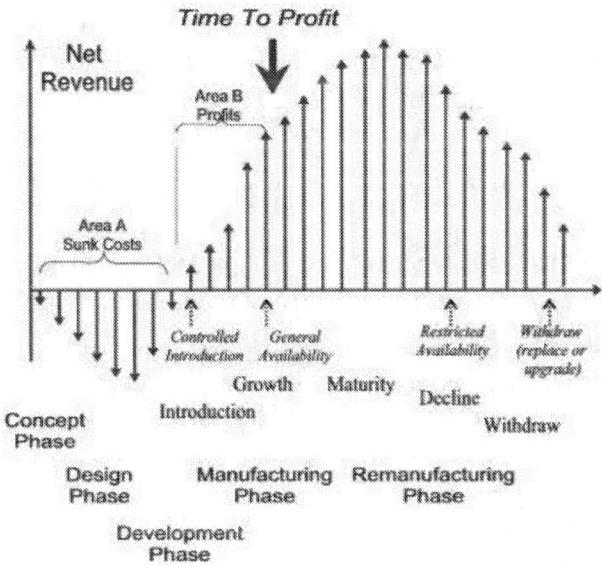

Business Mentors has researched over six hundred companies to identify the best practices that enable rapid Time to Profit. That is what this book is about—improving your

Time to Profit. You can develop profits in half the time. In three years, you can be twice as profitable as you are now.

The figure shows one example of a product development cycle and a product life cycle. While the words describing the phases may be different depending upon the industry and whether the offering is a service, a product, or a combination of both, the concepts are universal.

Our Philosophy

Our philosophy is that relevant practices are more important than best practices. Brevity is more important than academic discourse.

We will be only as academic as is necessary. We believe that that if an idea cannot be drawn on the back of a napkin or explained during an elevator ride, it is too complicated to be readily accepted by the employees.

In the late eighties when Ford said, "Quality is Job One!" everyone at Ford understood what that meant. It was a very succinct slogan. The fact that there would be training and statistical process control was not mentioned. The rallying cry was "Quality is Job One." The slogan became their compass, their North Star. Just as sailors need to know how to identify the Big Dipper and the North Star, let the models in this book be your North Star for marketing and sales.

This text is about more about what to do than how to do it. "How to" is training; "what to do" is information. Chances are you are already doing some of what this book is about. The appendix at the end of the text lists best practices from many industries. We strongly encourage you to creatively imitate or outright steal these ideas.

This is not a book where EBIT (Earnings before Interest and Taxes) or Asset Depreciation is discussed. It is a book about the meta-models used by marketing and sales staff. The meta-models used here will be customer focused.

Profit is good

Greed is not good. However, profit is good. We believe all good things come from profits: bonuses, stock options, higher pay scales, money to reinvest in the business and its employees, better medical benefits, and retirement plans.

Profitable companies can invest in their communities. Target, the discount retailer, reinvests 5 percent of its profits locally.

Profitable companies are great to work for. Xerox was in the sixties; Apple was in the seventies, and today, SAS in North Carolina is a great company to work for because it is profitable.

While there is no one magic bullet that will increase profitability, there are six bullets that will enable success. These are:

- ❏ The offering's features and attributes,
- ❏ Creating customer awareness,
- ❏ Positively impacting customer consideration,
- ❏ Being where the customers buy,
- ❏ Closing on the sale, and
- ❏ Having the customers **return.**

The magic occurs because of the synergy between the bullets.

Synergy is to Marketing and Sales as compound interest is to retirement planning. When soldiers are on a run, their footwork is such that they have to break cadence when crossing a bridge. Otherwise, the power of seventy-five feet coming down at once could collapse the bridge. There is power in being in step as many an old country bridge can attest

There is power when systems and processes are aligned to service the customer.

It is through the coherence of strategies and tactics that success becomes inevitable. Just as a laser beam is powerful because of the coherence and singularity of its wavelength, profitability is a result of the coherence of internal processes and systems.

The goal of this book is to provide an awareness of the three models that Marketing and Sales professionals use to make not only correct decisions, but also winning decisions.

Tsunami Process™

"We are an intelligent species and the use of our intelligence quite properly gives us pleasure. In this respect the brain is like a muscle. When it is in use we feel very good. Understanding is joyous."

—Carl Sagan (*Broca's Brain*, 1979)

The first model we shall look at is the Tsunami Process™. The Tsunami Process™ is customer-centric, meaning it focuses on the customer. The process is the result of a study of more than seventy-five companies. It differs from a product-focused model in that the emphasis is on thinking as customers do and then making decisions.

Tsunami Process™

Voice of Customer

↓

| The Offerings |
| Awareness |
| Consideration |
| Channels |
| Hit Rate |
| Repeat Purchase |

When IBM was slipping, it was because it was product focused, trying to create demand or **push** big "boxes." IBM CEO Lou Gerstner turned the company around by becoming customer focused and **providing solutions**. While reading this chapter, do your best to pretend that half of you is the customer.

Our Strength is also our Weakness

When researching companies, we discovered that each company had its own approach to looking at its businesses based on the functional strengths of its executives. We found that we could make predictions about a company's strategy based on what a new senior manager had done at his or her previous job.

Engineers look at the company one way. Often they want to improve the product. Marketing people look at the company another way. They create positive spin and will "sell" you.

In response to the problem of executive bias, we created a unified approach from the **Customer's Point of View.**

Why is this necessary? Why can't a new product launch manager simply focus on creating an offering that meets specifications? Why can't a CEO simply use the income statement and balance sheet to make decisions? There are many reasons:

- ❏ They could miss the fact that if a competitor is in five channels and their company is only in three, they could easily increase their company's revenues 60 percent simply by entering those other channels.

- ❏ They could miss the fact that a competitor has created a **reinforcing loop** to retain customers. For example, American Airlines provides frequent flyer miles by aligning itself with **many** partners. Use an AAdvantage Visa card and you get frequent flyer points. This encourages additional use of the airline. Delta Airlines provides its own frequent flyer miles and goes one step further. Delta provides free flights to Hawaii if you fly enough segments.

- ❏ There may be a "premium" channel that provides a unique advantage. Some channels provide high traffic of potential customers. Target, the discount retailer, now can be found on a tab of Amazon.com because Amazon.com has so much traffic. It is like having a storefront on a popular street.

- ❏ Some channels make life easier. In the eighties, one airline captured the bulk of an important channel—the travel agents—with its Sabre System. Instead of calling up several airlines, a travel agent could refer to a computer screen. The Sabre System made an agent's life easier and thus captured market share. Today many companies provide a **value-added service** to its channels to capture the channel. In return, the company asks for exclusivity.

- ❏ There may be a **premium feature**. The personal digital assistant, Palm, became popular because it easily shared data with a PC. It beat out Apple's Newton and all the Windows CE devices in the nineties.

The value of the Tsunami Process is that managers quickly realize the area they need to focus on so that their company can be more successful.

Voice of the Customer

The Tsunami Process™ starts with the voice of the customer, or VOC. The Voice of the Customer is commonly thought of as what the customer says. However, the Voice of the Customer is really three things:

❑ It is what the customer **expects**, but assumes you know. These are called **Implied** or **Basic Requirements**.

❑ It is what the customer can **state** or **request**. These are called **Expressed** or **Explicit Requirements**.

❑ Sometimes the customer has no idea of a feature or attribute. If the **customer has no words** for this until they see it, we call it a **Wow** or **Sizzle Requirement**.

At this point, is not essential to differentiate between the different classes of the Voice of the Customer, or VOC. That will be covered in the Kano Model chapter.

For now, let's assume the VOC consists of the typical things that customers can express. Marketing researchers capture this information in focus groups or through surveys. However, focus groups and surveys only capture the spoken or expressed VOC.

One important aspect of this stage in the process is to identify where your marketing and new product sponsors capture the Voice of the Customer. Often they lack a systematized approach to capturing spoken and written comments from customers and miss developing new products their customers want. When hunting ducks, you need to lead (aim where the ducks will be), not aim where the ducks are now. If you don't do that you miss the ducks. INTEL and 3M lead customers.

Starting with the VOC, the company can create an offering for its clients. The offering can be a product, a service, or a combination of both. As you examine the customers who are attracted to the offering, you will discover that they actually fall into segments. Market research segmentation and identifying the various needs of different segments can be used here to provide targeted offerings.

Different features and their price points will attract different customer segments. Let's pretend that due to its attributes or features, only 50 percent of the market will buy your offering. These features and attributes correspond to benefits for our customers. By modifying the attributes and features of our offering, you can capture additional market segments.

Use Features and Attributes to Attract Customers

Feature Set A Captures 50% of Market

Feature Set B Captures 75% of Market

How can you develop profits in half the time? One way is to identify those features or attributes that are easy to reproduce. Often having a common platform for your product enables this approach. In Europe, Electrolux of Sweden created the Euro-oven. The oven is based upon a common platform from which the company was able to produce forty-five different variants for the different needs of its European customers.

Awareness

It is not enough to have a product or a service for customers; the customers also need to be aware of it. Advertising creates awareness. Advertising media include: radio, TV, newspaper, direct mail (including postcards, billboards, electronic newsletters), Web sites, sales collateral, auto faxes, reviews by professionals in journals and newspapers, trade shows, and any other form of media that enables you to capture the attention of potential customers.

It seems obvious to say that if customers are not aware of your product or service, they will not purchase it. Yet engineers often fail to grasp the importance of Awareness. They seem to believe, "If we build it, they will come." That only works in the movies.

In the real world, customers need to know you exist in order to select you. This is sometimes referred to as being "on the customer's radar screen." We think of it as advertising.

For example, Xerox Corp., as reported in a book titled *The Force*, did not advertise in the Yellow Pages, a telephone business directory common in the United States. As a result, when an office wanted to purchase a copier, it could not find a Xerox salesperson. This situation was rectified in the nineties.

Consideration

Even though someone is aware of your offering they may not consider you. There are a number of reasons why someone will not consider you. They may:

- ❑ Presume you are too expensive,
- ❑ Have had a previous experience with your company that created a negative opinion,
- ❑ Have a false assumption of your capabilities, or
- ❑ Think you're too small, too large, too inexperienced, etc.

For example, in the nineties Xerox found that people would not buy their products because they considered them to be too expensive. Xerox launched an educational campaign, not to create awareness—everyone knew the Xerox name—but to alter potential customer's opinions. In 1994–5, radio and newspaper ads in North America emphasized the affordability of Xerox products and informed consumers that a Xerox copier could be purchased for as little as $99 a month. The campaign was a success.

Similarly, people assume that BMWs are too expensive. However, BMW now offers a sport utility vehicle that is in the same price range as other high-end sport utility vehicles. In Europe BMW offers a two-seater for approximately $9000.

So why doesn't a customer purchase your offering?

This question often falls to the sales force to answer. In addition to identifying the reasons customers are not purchasing your offering, you must study ways to overcome these problems. You may have to launch a marketing/advertising campaign to educate the customer.

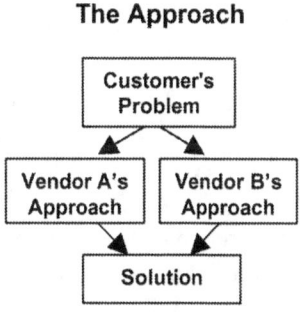

One way to get customers to consider your offering over competitor's offerings is to begin a campaign to educate them about the **benefits** of your approach. This is a presale activity, convincing stakeholders that your approach is better. Customers often jump to a solution based on past experience and what they are aware of in the marketplace. To make sure your offering is considered, you must be sure the customer has been educated.

If one cannot win a customer with a better approach than the competition, redefine the problem.

Every problem is nestled, like the rings of an onion, within another problem. Often you can help the customer solve a bigger problem where your product is a viable option. Clients will realize that what you are doing is self-serving, yet they will be grateful if you help them drain the swamp, rather than just kill the alligator climbing into their boat.

Redefining the Problem to Enable a New Solution

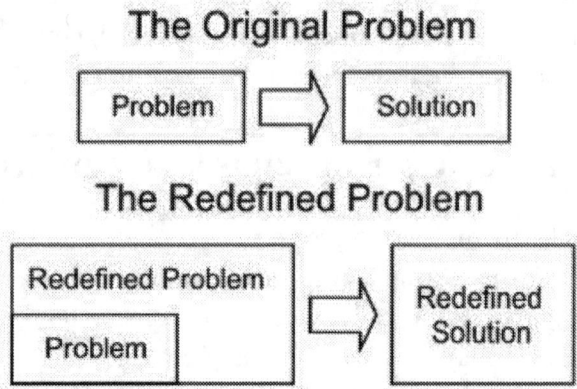

Assuming that your customers are **Aware** of and will **Consider** purchasing your offering, your task now is to make sure the offering is present in the **Channels of Distribution** in which your customers would commonly make a purchase.

For AT&T wireless phones, the channels consist of mall kiosks, storefronts, and the Web. Did we mention McDonald's? AT&T ran a campaign for its wireless services consisting of flyers at McDonald's that stated AT&T would contribute $25 to Ronald McDonald House for each purchase. Parents took note of the offering and sales increased.

Types of Channels

Channels can be either direct or indirect. **Direct Channels** are those in which the manufacturer sells directly to the customer. Examples of Direct Channels include: a direct sales force, a toll-free phone number, a factory showroom, and a manufacturer's catalog or Web site.

In an **Indirect Channel**, the customer does not deal directly with the manufacturer. Indirect Channels include retail stores, wholesalers, distributors, and value-added integrators. A category killer is a large retailer that has a specific focus in one area such as Staples does in office supplies or "Toys R Us" does in toys.

In the United States, Ingram's is a wholesaler to bookstores. Ingram's warehouses the books and then ships them to local bookstores. It also provides a software package to the bookstores it supports that makes ordering and inventory control easier.

Example: Simek's Expanded Using Channels

In the Midwest, Simek's started with selling meat and seafood to local area restaurants. Profits were fed, no pun intended, into retail stores. By 2005 its CEO hopes to have over twenty retail stores. Having a storefront helps to create brand awareness, enabling Simek's next step: grocery stores.

Today Simek's is working with more than one hundred local grocery stores. To accomplish this, Simek's created a well-advertised freezer section that contained thirty of its most popular products. The next step? Linking with 2,800 SuperAmerica convenience stores.[1]

Hit Rate or Closing Ratio

The **Hit Rate** or **Closing Ratio** is the percentage of sales closed when your offering is in front of the customer.

What helps with the customer decision?

Being a brand helps in differentiating your offering from the competition.

Sometimes it is **the package** that sells a product. In the discount channel, packaging is very important because the package provides the information that influences customers to make a decision.

Sometimes there are manufacturer or wholesaler representatives **in stores demonstrating** products. You often see this technique used in computer stores, food stores, and at trade shows. But the demonstrators are usually not sales staff. The key is motivating them to sell, not just demonstrate, the product. But how do you motivate them to sell? Give them compensation for every customer coupon that is redeemed at the cash register. This motivates both the demonstrator and the customer. It encourages the customer to purchase now, and, while the demonstrator may only receive $5 per coupon, it encourages him or her to sell more. Five dollars, the typical amount a cell phone kiosk representative earns when selling a phone, may not seem like much, but three of these an hour would double the income of many demonstrators.

A Motivated Sales Person—A True Story

In a Minneapolis January (minus two degree Fahrenheit), I got my gasoline and went in to pay and pick up a *Wall Street Journal*. The teenage clerk said, "Do you want a car wash?"

Is this kid for real? I thought. I replied, "Are you kidding? My car would turn into an ice cube!" The clerk said, "Oh you can use it at any time; [overcoming an objection] besides, I get a dollar for every one I sell [an innocent comment]." That kid was earnest and motivated. (And yes, I bought a car wash for use later. I remembered what it was like to be a teenager.)

Repeat Customers

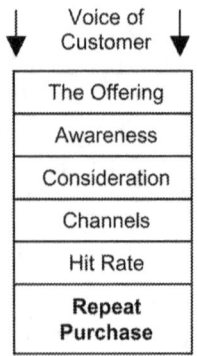

Once you have successfully obtained a customer, it is now important to make the customer a **Repeat Customer**. There are a number of strategies you can use to get a client to not only come back but also to turn him or her into an advocate or fan. These strategies will be discussed in greater detail in the chapter on customer satisfaction and customer loyalty.

The best practice of **co-branding**, putting two brands together, gets customers to come back more often. Gas stations sales have increased 40 percent since chains like Taco Bell set up shop inside the stations.

In some areas, Johnsonville Brats were sold through McDonald's, providing Johnsonville with a new channel, McDonald's with a brand-name product, and the customer with a known entity.

Customer Retention

Customer retention is critical to businesses both big and small. AT&T's long-distance service averages 70 million customers. Approximately two million customers join and two million drop every month. Given the expense of customers switching, imagine the benefit of even a 10 percent reduction in defections.

What are the telecoms trying to do? Their strategy is to provide a value-added bundle of services: local and long distance; personal 1-800 numbers; phone over cable TV; one cell phone number that works on several phones; high-speed Internet access; and one consolidated bill. Telecoms are trying to identify what the customers perceive as value and then provide it.

Research shows that customers come back when they are treated politely and fairly. Customers value good manners.

So what is the essence of the Tsunami Model? You begin by identifying both the customer's **Expressed** and **Unexpressed Needs**. Using this information, you create an offering. After an offering captures market share, you need to continually enhance the offering based upon the customer's feedback (**Voice of the Customer**). In addition, the customer needs to be **Aware** you exist, **Consider** you a viable option, find you in the **Channels** in which they shop, be sold on you (**Hit Rate**) when making the buying decision, and come back to you again and again (**Repeat Purchase**).

Key Point for Marketing and Sales Managers

The value of the Tsunami Process™, since it looks at your offering from the customer's point of view, is that it helps you identify what you need to do, rather what you have always done. Marketing and sales staff can quickly realize the area in which they need to focus so that they can be more successful.

If you want to increase profits, do you need to:
- ❑ Enhance the offering?
- ❑ Create awareness?
- ❑ Educate the channel or end user to consider you?
- ❑ Motivate the purchase decision through the channel, the end user, or both?
- ❑ Facilitate repeat purchases?

With limited budgets, choose what would help the most, not what you have the most comfort doing.

Kano

Voice of Customer

The Offerings
Awareness
Consideration
Channels
Hit Rate
Repeat Purchase

Kano Model

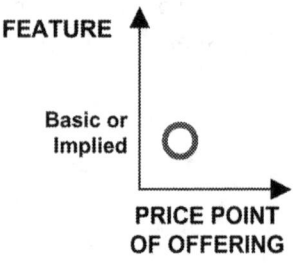

So how does one go about identifying what a customer wants? What should be the feature set in an offering? What should the channels receive?

Kano, of Japan, offers a three-tier model that impacts the Tsunami Process in the areas of the Offering and Consideration.

Basic Features and Attributes

The first level of the model is **Basic Quality**. Also called **Implied Quality** and **Implied Requirements**, it consists of those features or attributes that are essential and should always be present.

They are so basic that the customer assumes they will be present. Examples of Basic Quality include: car windows that go up and down; a toaster with settings; a car service appointment unmarred by grease on the dashboard or steering wheel.

As is shown in the figure above, when you offer Basic Quality you are typically competing in a commodity business. For a "new" product to be successful it needs to be a Low Cost Leader. Otherwise the product or offering needs to be enhanced in such a way as to provide either a perceived or actual value from the customer's point of view.

For example, to maintain the perception of lowest price, Wal-Mart identifies the one hundred best-selling medications in a geographic area and then makes sure that its store's price on these medications is the lowest. Customers will assume that Wal-Mart is the low cost leader on other medications, but it is probably only true on these one hundred or so.

Wal-Mart advertising shows a happy face with prices dropping 25 percent. The subconscious notices the percentage even if the conscious mind does not.

As you move beyond the first level of Basic Quality, or Implied Requirements, it is important not to forget what is considered basic from the customers' point of view. If you fail to deliver what the customer thought was basic, they will be very upset and feel ripped off. One retailer of suits offered a high quality suit for $300, but the slacks were an additional $100. Their redefinition of a suit, a jacket sans trousers, caused many customers to leave the store.

Dissatisfied customers will relate their experience to twenty of their friends.

The Expressed Voice of the Customer

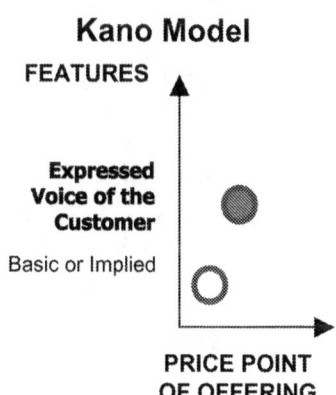

Kano Model
FEATURES

Expressed Voice of the Customer

Basic or Implied

PRICE POINT OF OFFERING

Dr. Kano's second level is called the **Expressed Voice of the Customer**. Here the customer can state what they want. Marketing research is useful here. New product managers need to remember what the customers considered basic—in addition to capturing what the customer expressly stated he or she wanted.

When clients ask for certain things, whether part of a service or a specific feature, you are in the realm of the spoken **Voice of the Customer**. The automobile industry is at the forefront of using market research to identify what the customer wants and how much they will pay for it. Niche players can succeed through enhancing an offering or filling a void to capture market share.

Niche Player Survival

There are four reasons **Niche Players** typically succeed here.

First, there can be a barrier that prevents other companies from entry, such as having to get FDA approval, or not having the engineering diagrams to service certain types of equipment.

Second, the threat of competition can be low, as when in possession of a patent.

Third and most commonly, the niche player often accepts a lower price because it has a lower cost of business.

Last but not least, another company can create a niche player. If you want to decrease your competitor's revenue, why not set up a niche player to compete in a high margin area?

Consumables are often in the 50 to 75 percent profit range so anything you do in that area to reduce a competitor's revenue can be very successful.

Wow, Sizzle, and Excitement

When you add excitement or sizzle you can capture long-term market share if it is patentable. Intel and 3M are constantly pushing the envelope by providing new and superior offerings to the marketplace. For example, Post-Its® patented sticky adhesive cannot be copied for seventeen years, providing 3M with an ensured revenue stream.

Kano Model
FEATURES

Wow and Sizzle

Expressed Voice
of the Customer

**Basic or
Implied**

**PRICE POINT
OF OFFERING**

In this category you can redefine a business, as Starbucks did with coffee, or create a new category, as Chrysler did with minivans.

Providing delightful attributes and features enable you to charge a premium. Eventually those **Wow, Sizzle, and Excitement** attributes and features become part of the customer's lexicon.

If you cannot patent it, rest assured you will be copied.

When Ford introduced a charge card that enabled the customer to save on future car purchases, GM launched its own credit card within eight months.

A Feature That Wowed Parents

When a water connection was put on the **outside** of the refrigerator door, parents squealed with delight. They knew that containers were no longer going to be knocked over and there would be fewer spills to clean up.

A Tale of Four Newspapers—Service That Sizzles

In our Pittsburgh, PA office, the employee receives four newspapers: *Wall Street Journal*, the *New York Times*, the *Pittsburgh Post Gazette*, and the local *Tribune Review*.

All arrive between 5:30 and 6:00 a.m. All arrive in a plastic bag.

The *Wall Street Journal* and *Tribune Review* are on the grass or in the snow, about twenty feet from the door. (Getting the paper in the snow is a dissatisfier.)

The *New York Times* and *Post Gazette* are always on the doorstep! (A nice feature anytime and a Wow feature when raining.)

If there is any precipitation, the *New York Times* is double wrapped in two plastic bags, put on in reverse order to make sure no snow or rain can get into the paper. That Sizzles!

When the employee was told we would not reimburse for the local papers, guess which one she dropped? Guess who got a $20 tip each year and who got a $5 tip.

Wow Often Meets an Unexpressed Need

When P&G entered the Japanese market in 1995 it first sent out researchers to study Japanese dishwashing rituals. They learned that the Japanese housewife typically squirted out more detergent than was needed. Robert A. McDonald, head of P&G's Japanese operations, reported it was "a clear sign all of frustration." This was a sign of an unarticulated consumer need.[2]

Wow is the New York Times being **double bagged**—covered with two plastic sleeves facing opposite directions when it rains to make sure it does not get wet.

The minivan, not a car and not a van, was a Wow product. Wow features can create new categories as Palm did in Personal Digital Assistants and Xerox did in copiers.

If you are the first one to the marketplace with a Wow offering, you can become the new category.

Wow service can lead to customer loyalty when emotions are involved. When tornados hit Camile, GA, a sales associate got Capital One to grant its one thousand credit card holders two months free from payments. These customers will probably be loyal for life.

Often, meeting an unexpressed need can result in a new business.

Do you remember Jiffy Mix? While in college it really stretched a student's budget. The original Jiffy Mix comes from the privately held Chelsea Milling Company.

Mabel White Homes created Jiffy Mix in 1930. Her family had been milling flour since 1802 and Jiffy was a sideline at first. What prompted her to create the product? She met an unexpressed need. She noticed that a local widower had made biscuits for his son that were, well, hard! Mabel decided to create mix that "even a man could make." The result was the now-familiar blue box. With over sixteen products, Jiffy Mix is number one in product placement, but not in revenue. How can that be possible? The company charges less per box.

For New Product Managers

The problems facing Marketing and Sales staff are twofold. First, the **Basic Quality** attributes need to be identified. **Basic Quality**, also referred to as **Implied Requirements**, is often missed. Clients do not mention these requirements because they are "obvious." They expect a car with windshield wipers and a cup holder. Missing an Implied Requirement is a major cause of rework. Too often we have seen products introduced without basic features.

For example, companies have tried to offer:
- ❑ A printer without print drivers. It only sold twenty-five units.
- ❑ A service of printing colored overheads that looked black on the screen. The colors used were opaque, not transparent.

Capturing Basic or Implied Quality

How do you identify the unspoken requirements? Sometimes it is obvious. For example, when President Kennedy said he wanted to put a person on the moon by the end of the decade, it was understood that NASA had to bring the astronauts back! It was an Implied Requirement. Some Implied Requirements are not so obvious. To capture these:
- ❑ Look at your scars. Where have you failed to meet the customer requirements before?
- ❑ Use Benchmarking. Create a list of attributes or features offered by the competition.
- ❑ Understand what the customer had with the old offering before it was replaced by the new.

Remember the End User

One software user group complained that it now took seven screens to do what used to take two. The End Users were very unhappy with the "new" product. Remember: End Users are customers too.

Beware Technology for Technology's Sake

The second issue for project and new product managers concerns providing Wow and Sizzle for the sake of Wow and Sizzle.

Avoid technology for technology's sake. Technology is about providing a solution that makes the customer's life easier or that makes the product more effective. Too often Information Technology personnel provide Wow and Sizzle without providing what the customers requested. The customers didn't get what they requested, but a software programmer is very pleased with him-or herself.

The Bottom Line

If you want to know what your deliverables should be, look at it from the *customers' point of view* and provide an offering that always meets the customer's unspoken expectations, consistently meets their specific requests, and whenever possible, provides them with delight. It is not expensive to provide WOW to the customer—**simply observe them and watch for the unexpressed need.** If you do not know what Wow or Sizzle looks like from the Customer's Point of View, under promise and over deliver.

Approaches are discussed in the Architectures chapter.

Awareness

"It's called the three foot rule. Anybody within three feet of your employees should know about your offering and its benefits. That is the best advertising you can do."

Kobi James

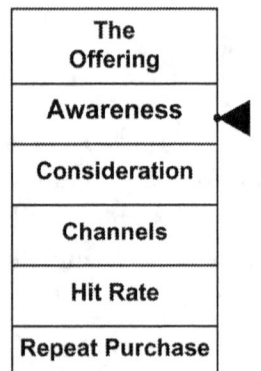

Awareness is the second key to successful profit growth.

The first Sunday of the year, the Minnesota version of the *New York Times* includes a fifty-page brochure on the joys of taking a "Winter Break" in Chicago. Chicago promotes itself, including information on stores, theatres, restaurants, museums, and special events.

Chris Zane, owner of a Branford, Connecticut bicycle shop, bought the Yellow Pages ad and phone number of a nearby competitor when it went out of business. Over the next month, 285 calls to the defunct business were connected through to him, and his sales rose by 40 percent.[3] Don't think it's easy to double profits? It is easy if the customer is aware of you!

Nokia gave the winners of the fifty-first Emmy Awards a Nokia 8800 cell phone, priced at over US$700 each. Nokia can hardly wait until these movers and shakers are seen using their phones at restaurants and in *National Inquirer* photos.

Pfizer Inc. took out an ad for Viagra, a medication for erectile dysfunction, in an automobile magazine. As men wait for new tires to be put on their cars, they read the motor magazine and come across the ad. It was 2.5 pages long, so it was hard to miss.

It is not enough to have a product or a service for customers. Customers also need to be aware of it. Awareness is what clients typically think of as advertising. Many a new software startup and engineering concern have failed because they did not budget for marketing.

Awareness Technique for Services

One way professional service providers create awareness is by giving talks and seminars to business people. Expertise Marketing, of Concorde, Mass., sent surveys to 8,500 professional practices across the United States. Lawyers, accountants, business consultants, health care specialists, and others were surveyed to see how they promoted their practices effectively.[4] The professional practices surveyed ranged from under $5 million in revenue to the largest national and international firms. Only a third could state with certainty that they gained new clients and new revenue from their promotions, reported Susan Lowe, president of Expertise Marketing.

So what produced the best results? The free sample. Seminars held by firms on their own behalf ranked as the most effective of all promotional vehicles at bringing in new clients, even though they were used by only 54.4 percent of the respondents.

One of the most successful educational products Business Mentors has seen is Successful Money Management®. This is a product, normally licensed to accountants and certified financial planners, which educates their potential clients on financial matters. Typically presented in three, three-hour segments, the material provides a strong foundation for potential clients to understand the basics of financial risk and reward.

At the end of the seminar a free financial analysis is provided for those interested. Potential clients were exposed to the expertise of the presenters and **trust** developed over the three presentations. It is not uncommon for 50 percent or more of the participants to request a financial analysis. And this leads them to purchase the product.

Who Really Needs to Be Aware?

Choosing how to create Awareness is an exercise in creativity and this is the primary reason ad agencies are worth their weight in gold.

We can create Awareness directly with the customer, the channel of distribution to the consumer, or a major influencer.

Haggar Clothing Company decided to advertise its expensive men's black label line only in women's magazines. Why? Its market research showed that women either buy for, or accompany their husbands 89 percent of the time a menswear purchase is made in a department store. Since women make or influence the decisions, why not market to them? The ads used "hunks and humor" that appealed to women, and didn't offend men.

AT&T advertised its cellular phones in McDonald's restaurants in 1997. It realized that single parents were especially in need of a way for their children to contact them.

In the fall of 1999 a full-page ad for the Palm Pilot showed the Amazon.com Web site on the screen. The ad subtly indicated that the Palm was wired to the Internet and also created additional awareness for Amazon.com as a site.

Awareness can take different forms. Today it is popular to buy naming rights to stadiums. H.J. Heinz Co. will pay $57 million dollars over ten years to name the new Pittsburgh Steelers and University of Pittsburgh Panthers football stadium on Pittsburgh's north shore. Having both college and NFL football teams playing guarantees Heinz will have more airtime. The company also got the stadium to agree to use only Heinz ketchup.

Awareness consists of all the sales collaterals and advertising one provides. It includes favorable reviews in technical or trade journals. It consists of "buzz" and contests. It also consists of branding.

One Executive MBA program had classes on the weekend. Its Web site looked very friendly. Its classes were taught by professors from a well-known local MBA school. Its very existence and its brand identity were linked to this well-known MBA school. But you wouldn't know it to look at the Web site. It was recommended that the program change its folksy Web site to look like the Web site of the parent program. Also, the Web site was under the program's name, not the parent's name. It was recommended that it purchase a dot-com address so that it could be found on search engines.

Case Study

Let's look at the circles below and identify the end users and channels of a new business venture. The company was in the business of putting hitches onto cars and trucks.

How did the company's sales and marketing staff create awareness? They took out an ad in the Yellow Pages. They estimated that perhaps 25 percent of their potential customers knew about the company.

The company was in one channel: direct sales. How could they increase awareness? They brainstormed a number of different ways.

	% of Channels that were aware	% of customers who were aware
Name of Offering A service that attaches hitches to cars and trucks	0%	25%

If the awareness level is not acceptable, what could you do? Below is what they came up with.

Partner with new car dealers	Recommend a friend program	Advertise in bike magazines
Yellow Page ads e.g., bikes	Booth at local boat show	Advertise in fishing magazines

Other Examples

A CPA firm used this analysis and decided to focus on building relationships with bankers. The bankers often knew which companies were growing and seeking loans and could pass along this information to the local CPA firm.

To make sure end users select products with Intel microprocessors, Intel sales and marketing promotes their chips directly to consumers even though PC manufacturers are the actual purchasers of the product. They wanted to influence consumers with their "Intel Inside" campaign, because consumers often rely on the stores' customer service people to offer recommendations. Maybe you have seen their silver-suited dancers or the Blue Man Group advertising the Pentium line. Intel pays vendors to have the Intel Inside® trademark clearly displayed.

The AFLAC duck has created tremendous awareness for the company. Introduced in 2000, awareness went from 2 percent to 80 percent.[5][6] In 2001 the commercial featured the duck on a roller coaster. AFLAC linked the advertisement to a tie in with eighteen Six Flags wooden roller coasters. The  commercial was shown on the monitors by the rides and an ALFAC "quack" was sounded at the beginning of each ride. AFLAC sales persons brought ducks to leave with clients. (It was a door opener.) Remember, this was an awareness commercial. Would you consider buying AFLAC's services? Have they communicated a benefit of using their services to you?

Both Intel and AFLAC applied the best practice of using a common theme over extended periods of time to create Awareness.

What happens when you stop investing in Awareness?

Plymouth stopped advertising and sales dropped from 400,000 to 300,000 units.

When Dr. Pepper stopped advertising, the brand almost disappeared. Fortunately, its advertising group had excellent Product Placement by having Tom Hanks drink some Dr. Pepper in the hit movie *Cast Away*.[7]

Apply this to Yourself

Now shade in the area that indicates the percentage of potential stakeholders (distributors, channels, and customers) that are aware of your offering.

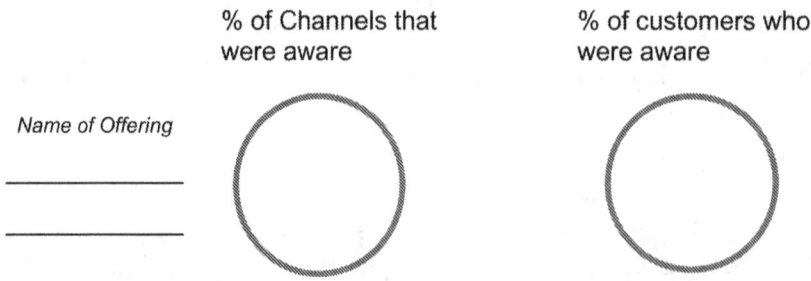

Name of Offering

_____

_____

% of Channels that were aware

% of customers who were aware

If the awareness level is not acceptable, what could you do?

_____   _____   _____

_____   _____   _____

_____   _____   _____

Notes to Myself:

Examples of ways to create Awareness are all around us.

❑ A gas station sponsors the local little league. The fifteen tykes promote good will for the station. **Who should you use as bulletin boards?**

❑ A publisher of city maps uses high school bands to sell its product as a fundraiser. This approach was so popular that it became a new channel for the publisher. **What special interest group could promote awareness for your offerings**?

❑ What Web sites would like to cross-link with you? Could any of these become a channel?

The Silly Putty brand languished until it was mentioned in the *NY Times* and became a hit. **What journalists need to write a favorable comment on your offering?**

Perhaps Awareness is not an issue for you. Everyone knows Xerox. Over 60 percent of PC owners know what Yahoo is (for non-PC users it drops to 20 percent). And 99.9 percent of MBA graduates from the top ten schools know that a BMW is a car. They may not know what the letters stand for, but they know of the vehicle.

Next Steps

Using the approach on the previous page, do you need to create additional awareness? Is that the key to doubling your profits? Or is it something else—like Consideration, the topic of the next chapter?

To create Awareness you have many venues. Remember to:

❑ Choose the venue that your customer will see or hear. Advertise where your customers read. Provide messages on the stations they watch or listen to.

❑ Identify Early Adopters and have them use your offering.

❑ Target the Influencers—those who write or talk about your offering. Pay them to promote your product or encourage them to put in a good word.

Note to New Product Managers

Awareness is sometimes thought of as Branding. In this text, Branding is more than Awareness.

Do you prefer Sony or Sanyo? GM or Toyota? Motel 8 or the Marriott?

The best brands create an emotional awareness. A brand is a promise. While Awareness puts you on the customer's radar screen, it is Branding that leads clients to a purchase decision.

New product mangers should also consider positive reinforcing loops. Kohl's sales increased the last quarter of 2001. After the September 11, 2001 terrorist attack, the business world said sales would drop. What happened? Kohl's increased advertising. It also had a reinforcing loop, a customer loyalty program to encourage additional purchases. The more you buy, the better the deals you can get.

Consideration

If they believe it is true, it is true.

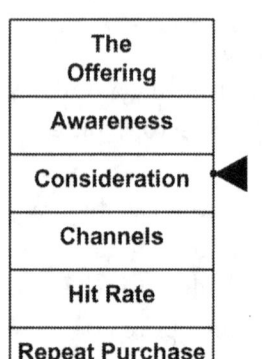

The Offering
Awareness
Consideration
Channels
Hit Rate
Repeat Purchase

Your success depends on your customers considering your offering to be a viable option. You may have a good product or service and the customers may be aware you exist; however, if there are negative connotations associated with your company or offering, they will not make a purchase.

What Do You Think of Me?

If you had to purchase a printer, would you prefer a NEC printer or a Hewlett-Packard?

If you had to purchase a computer, would you prefer a GE or a Dell?

If you had to purchase a doll, would you prefer Harley Davidson doll or just about anyone else? You laugh. Harley Davidson is known for motorcycles. Yet there is now a Biker Barbie®. Harley Davidson wanted to soften the image of Harley to entice more women to purchase their motorcycles and thus co-branded a doll with Mattel.

Potential customers may be Aware of your existence, but there may be other factors associated with your offering that prevent them from considering it for a purchase. You may be considered:

- ❑ Too expensive—BMW or Ford?
- ❑ Too Cheap—Imitation or a real diamond?
- ❑ As having poor service—Mystery Motels or the Hyatt?
- ❑ As having poor quality—Tijuana watches or department store watches?

Consideration Can Work in Your favor

Examples include:

- ❑ Having a feature or attribute the customer really wants, such as the Maytag Gemini range. It has two ovens so you can cook dishes at different temperatures.

❑ An e-commerce site that permits the return of a purchase to a brick and mortar store.

❑ A vendor's sales representative that also sends clients your way.

❑ Having Oprah make your book the Book of the Month. (Too late now; she quit.)

A Brand Has Associations

Your brand identity has associations that impact how you are considered. The "five and dime" tradition of the early 1900s is carried forward today with the "dollar store." How much do you expect to pay if you go into a Dollar Tree store?

Kaufmanns, a retail store in Pittsburgh, PA, always has a big after Thanksgiving Day sale. The store also provides an area where children can buy presents for their parents away from the parent's watchful eyes. The children are given a slip with how much they can spend and then elves help them select the gifts. Thus Kaufmanns has become a part of many families' holiday tradition. You can find three generations of parents who have taken their children to Kaufmanns. Grandmas will talk about how their mothers used to take them on the trolley car to Kaufmanns so they could buy a dress during the Thanksgiving sale.

Wal-Mart is considered to be "the low cost leader." Wal-Mart does not let chance determine what their customers believe about them. They actively tell the customer to think of them as the low cost leader.

The Dayton's (of Dayton Hudson and Target fame) in Minneapolis has a flower show in the spring. It is an event and family tradition that indicates the subzero weather is gone.

Kohl's is the brand name low price clothing store.

These companies present a consistent brand to their customers. They try to **become a positive part of their customer's lives.**

It helps to tell customers what you want them to consider you to be. To do this you need to explain the benefits, not the features.

Intel advertisements showed people in stylized clean room suits called bunny suits. But even as Awareness went up, it didn't impact Consideration. Computer manufacturers turned to lower cost AMD chips. When asked, computer store clerks had to explain honestly that sometimes the difference between AMD and Intel was the price. Lower cost AMD chips stole market share. So in 1998 Intel commercials showed the value of fast processor speeds. These commercials were easy for the non-technical person to understand.

They showed a person jumping out of a plane watching the ground appear as his chute slowly, much too slowly, opened. Guess who makes chips for PCs that are fast? Intel!

The concept was so good that two years later, AT&T@Home copied the Intel marketing idea to promote and explain the value of cable modems to its cable users. AT&T@Home showed the advantage of a cable modem in newspaper ads with the picture of a rocket filling the computer screen after one second, compared to a second screen in which just one-quarter of the picture had appeared after sixty seconds using a standard phone modem.

Which would you rather have?

After one second: After 60 seconds:

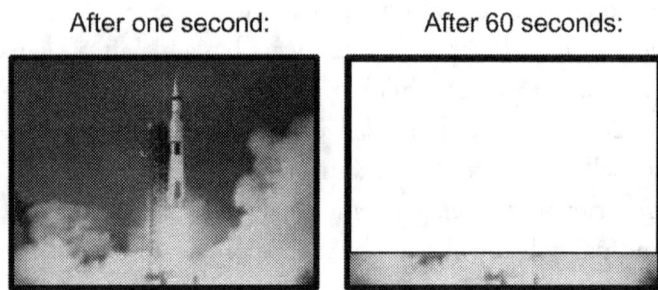

Consideration involves explaining the benefits of your offering's features and attributes in way the customer can understand. Who cares if the MTBF, or mean time before failure, of a light bulb is 37,000 hours? Show a commercial of a student entering college, and then show the student graduating and unscrewing the light bulb to take with him. Now the customer understands what *long lasting* really means! You will lose the **Consideration** battle when you fail to point out to the customer what you want them to believe about you.

You will also stop being considered if you quit offering the customer a feature or attribute they really want. K-Mart lost market share when it stopped selling women's slacks with an elastic waist. K-Mart regained share when it reintroduced the reliable, practical clothes its core customers wanted. Who were its core customers? Mothers who wanted slacks with the elastic waistband!

Consideration is the third key to successful profit growth. Even if customers know about your offering, would they consider you?

Common Issues That Minimize Consideration

Why are they not considering you? Is it a lack of faith in your competence, the life cycle cost, service after the sale, quality or reliability? When you know the answer to this question, you can address the issue through advertising, education, or other means. For example, a Midwest HVAC installer and repair service found that customers would not Consider them because they were not "Honeywell certified."

The company changed their promotional material to stress their many certifications along with the experience of their people and their state licenses. They began to win bids.

Two Approaches to Consideration: Firestone / Ford Explorer

In August 2000 Firestone faced a recall on tires mainly used on the Ford Explorer. The story made national news. Eight months later Bridgestone/ Firestone Inc. launched the biggest advertising campaign in its history. Firestone's research showed that customers, especially women, did not trust the company. Firestone ads reassured consumers of the safety of their tires. Firestone told customers that they are dedicated to "making it right."

On the other hand, Ford's research found that customers were not worried about the Explorer as long as it did not have Firestone tires on it. Ford promoted the positive experiences drivers can have if they purchase an Explorer. Two companies involved in the same crisis were presenting very different views to alter customers' perceptions and thus their Consideration.

Case Study: Wendy's

There's no point in running a national campaign if it does not work. When Penny's ran ads in the eighties, the products might not be in the stores because local managers had the final authority on product placement, regardless what the national ads might say.

This was finally corrected in the nineties.

Some of Wendy's stores have had later hours. By 2001, 90 percent of the Wendy's outlets were open late, so it was then safe to roll out a nationwide campaign. The goal was to create Awareness and Consideration for the late-night stop. They never mentioned their competition, but think for a moment: what other Brand is open late?

Denny's is open late. Wendy's had to compete with Denny's.

The ads started with Dave Thomas, Wendy's founder, talking to a young man asleep in front of the TV. "Wake up!" Mr. Thomas demanded. A voice-over ad mentions that "Wendy's pickup window is open late." The commercial illustrates the desired behavior of the customer, showing him going to Wendy's and driving home with a bag of burgers.

It is very direct and states exactly what Wendy's wants the customer to consider.

Key Point

If Consideration is keeping your customers away, you need to find out why by asking them. Do a survey of lost sales. Find out the real reason. Then take action to change the customer's Consideration of your offering.

As a marketing or sales manager, you must understand that your company does have an image or brand. Even if it is unplanned, it exists. It may support or discourage customers from considering your offering. If necessary you may need to separate yourself from your parent company, as Lexus and Infinity did from their parents.

Last but not least, your channels of distribution have an image. Does their image help or hurt you?

Channels

There is a story of an old mountain man who was lost in a Colorado winter blizzard when he stumbled into an old miners' shack. It was empty and in need of repair. There was a large cast iron stove there. He saw the stove and said to it, "Give me heat."

The stove replied, "Give me wood!" The man was exhausted and did not feel like doing any additional work. So he angrily replied, "Give me heat and I'll give you some wood."

The stove was bad tempered and replied, "Give me wood and I'll give you heat."

The man did not give any wood to the stove and he froze in his sleep. The stove, without a fire, slowly rusted away.

Vendors and channels sometimes treat each other this way.

As we discuss channels of distribution, recognize that the company and the distributor each provide benefits to the other. Together we must be better off than if we work alone in service to the customer. If this is not true, another company will discover a better way to meet the customers' needs.

There is an advantage to being the first to discover a new channel.

Channels should provide advantage

The Offering
Awareness
Consideration
Channels ◄
Hit Rate
Repeat Purchase

The goal is to be in the channels where your customers shop. The more channels in which your offering is present, the more you sell. When the customer cannot locate you in the channel where they are shopping, they are likely to choose a substitute.

A "Channel" is the route a product takes from the manufacturer (or producer) to the end user (or customer). In the United States, farmers often sell directly to the customer via roadside stands. L.L.Bean, a catalogue retailer, also uses a direct channel.

An indirect channel has intermediaries. For example, Cadbury manufactures its Big Turk chocolate bar in London and delivers it to wholesalers, who sell it to retail stores such as Sobeys, and Sobeys sells it to you.

Direct Merchandising refers to selling directly to the customer. Examples include: street vendors, Internet vendors, direct mail (including catalogues, magazine ads, and telemarketing). Indirect Merchandising refers to selling via intermediaries, such as value-added resellers; wholesalers, which often warehouse the products; and retailers. Retailers vary from big box stores, which are often category killers; small boutiques; wholesale clubs like Costco; discount retailers like Wal-Mart and Target; and theme retailers, such as the magic store or the used athletic equipment store.

Sometimes you can make a channel an advantage. Dell Computer uses the direct sale channel as a cost effective strategy when combined with their Build-to-Order business model.

The trend in the future will be for more sales in the direct channel to reduce costs and eliminate the middle man. This is due in large part to the quality movement. Both the Web and Reverse Auctions will reduce the need of sales staff except in cases where the customer perceives sales as a provider of value-added services. Sales support is often taken over by Customer Service Representatives. The more complex the offering, the more sales and customer support staff will be needed.

This is why computer and server manufacturers use Value-Added Resellers, or VARs. They take over the Customer Service support. Large distributors, such as Ingram Micro, provide engineering and technical support to the Value-Added Resellers.

The channel that is most efficient will have a price advantage. The customer will be drawn to use whatever is easiest for the customer.

Customer Maturity

All customers are not created equal. Some have more knowledge and experience.

Inexperienced customers need explanations and handholding. Whether it is a vendor's biomechanical engineer working alongside a physician during a hip replacement surgery, or a Gateway sales representative explaining the different configurations to the customer at a Gateway Country store—some clients need help.

When Hewlett Packard first sold gas chromatographs, the salesperson had to explain the concept and column material. Later, as part of their BS degree, chemists were trained in gas chromatography and needed less support. As the chemist's curriculum matured, the chemist's needs shifted. This particular customer became the expert and knew more than the salesperson. Today a chemist calls a 1-800 number to place an order.

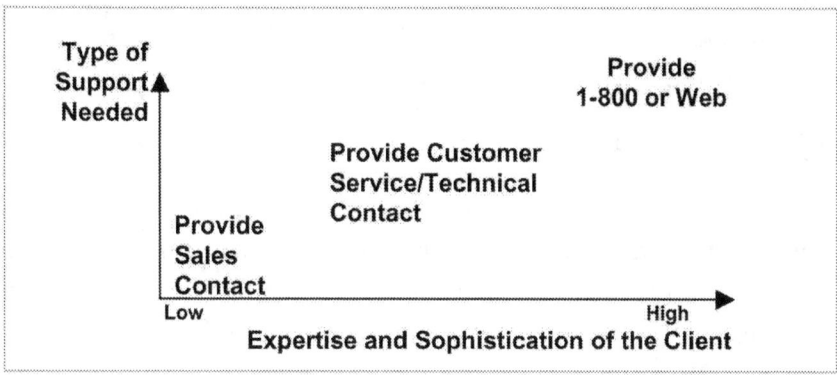

So periodically we need to look at the customers and decide how to best support them. The less expertise the customer has, the more support the customer will need.

The goal is not to reduce support to save money, but rather to provide support to the customer in a way that is of maximum benefit to the customer.

Beware of getting ahead of your customers. Several computer manufacturers incorrectly believed "Everything is going to the Web" and "took" their resellers' clients. The resellers looked overseas and partnered with new manufacturers.

Avon added Channels the right way

Avon is calling, just not at home. The direct sales retailer of women's cosmetics is adding channels. Kiosks were introduced in the United States in 1998. In addition to kiosks, Avon Products, Inc. negotiated with J.C. Penney to place a "store-within-a-store" at the retailer.

The strategy is intended to enable Avon to access new customers that the company is not currently reaching. Andrea Jung, Avon's president and chief executive officer, reported to analysts: "The store-within-a-store concept is an evolution of Avon's 115-year heritage of building relationships with women in innovative ways. While direct selling will always be our principal sales channel, expanding access to new customers will help accelerate top-line growth."

Dell Computer began to use kiosks in the fall of 2001 to reach consumers. They sensed this Channel would lead to a new segment. It was part of their launch to capture the consumer PC market and it included an $899 PC.

Avoiding Channel Conflict

The Avon Lady will not be going away. Ms. Jung also emphasized that the products to be sold in the store-within-a-store are from a **completely different product line** from the one sold by Avon representatives in the company's sales brochure. "The products in the Avon brochure will always be the domain of the Avon representative," Ms. Jung said. The store line is priced significantly higher than the core Avon products.

This is just the opposite of the friction that Intel and Compaq felt with their resellers. Intel pulled back from direct selling its NetStructure e-commerce brand and now sells through its Original Equipment Manufacture, or OEM partners. Similarly, "Compaq bowed to the pressure of channel partners and softened a direct sales model a few years ago."[8]

Why do companies try to take customers from their channels? First, it is to improve their bottom line by eliminating the percentage the channel gets. Second, it is based on the assumption that the customer's experience and sophistication has increased, making the channel redundant.

When a manufacturer is new, it has to sell a channel on offering their products. As time goes on, the channel needs to sell the manufacturer on its importance to the manufacturer's success.

With over 500,000 Avon ladies in the United States, Avon has been careful to partner with them. For example, the direct sales representatives were given the opportunity to run the mall kiosks. Avon also has 16,000 sales representatives signed up as Web or e-representatives

The Avon e-commerce site allows customers to choose a local representative or to purchase from Avon directly. The e-representatives use personalized Web pages to communicate with their customers, receive and process orders for products, check product availability and shipping status, create and send customer invoices, make payments to Avon, and manage other aspects of their Avon business on-line.

Value Added by Using the Avon Lady

Why use an Avon lady? One reason is to **receive the merchandise while you are at home.** For another, Avon launched its "Beauty Representatives" initiative in July 2000. The Avon representative can **provide the value-added services of beauty consultation and makeovers.** To ensure quality, Avon provided training that included self-study, a test, and then two days in class to actually practice creating makeovers.

Note to Marketing Managers

If the Avon lady can expand into additional channels, so can you. What channels can you expand into?

How can you differentiate the offerings to minimize channel conflict?

Always remember that your goal is to be the compelling choice for your channel partner and your customer.

Hit Rate

Customers buy from trusted individuals of retailers. Offerings don't just sell themselves.

We will not discuss how to sell or how to close; there are excellent courses on those topics.

The Offering
Awareness
Consideration
Channels
Hit Rate ◀
Repeat Purchase

However, there are several best practices that are not yet in common practice

Modeling

Roche Pharmaceuticals does it. Xerox does it. What is it? Modeling! They bring together three of their top salespersons on a specific product and then ask them questions. *Fortune Magazine* reported that when Len Vickers went from the United States to England to run Rank Xerox Sales and Marketing, he asked why some nationalities were buying more of a certain product than other nationalities. He had a team identify how certain products were sold and then shared the information across Western Europe.

Modeling includes understanding both the thoughts and strategies a sales person is using, in addition to physical items such as sales collaterals.

How do you position your offering? What is your Unique Selling Proposition?

What sales letters and sales script do you use?

What needs are really being fulfilled for the clients?

What are you thinking as you sell?

The questions are designed to take the unconscious and make it conscious. From this information skills and sales aids are discerned. Then a course is created and rolled out to the troops.

Smaller companies can use the same approach. Unfortunately, sales staffs are often competitive and salespersons focus on personal bonuses. To encourage the sharing of information, reward the mentor with a percentage of the increased revenue the sales mentees generate.

Inside Sales Strategies

To find the best practices one need only enter a Circuit City or Best Buy. Circuit City provides staff training over the Internet using high-speed connections. Management makes sure personnel know their products.

The inside sales staff helps customers when they shop. "Need CD-ROMs with the new PC? How about a three-year worry-free repair warranty covering parts and labor?"

The staff also helps the store against loss. The inside sales staff is rewarded for reduced shrinkage.

Sell Collaterals—Inside Sales Strategy

It is hard to get a customer these days, so it makes sense to maximize the revenue stream from the ones you have. One way is to sell additional services or products with your offering. Timing is everything. While they are in the buying mood, sell them the additional support they need. Let's look at some leaders' best practices.

With clothing priced 20 to 30 percent below retail, the Men's Warehouse trains its staff in pairing accessories to the suits. This practice is now a common way in retail to gather additional revenue. Do your sales or service personnel sell additional "accessories?" How do you measure that?

At CompUSA you can buy a printer and leave the store without a printer cable. They would ask if you needed one at Circuit City.

As part of its 1998 strategy, Best Buy wanted its staff to sell accessories. That is not what they call it, but the idea is the same. They retrained their sales force to sell more to the customer by "having more of a customer focus." If you buy a video camera, expect them to suggest (try to sell you) a cable. Buy a PC, and expect to be reminded about keyboard covers and discs. At Best Buy you will leave the store with all the material you need.

Customer Service at AOL:

When you call for customer service at AOL you can expect to have an additional service suggested. When AOL and Time Warner merged, the AOL customer service representatives sometimes attempted to cross-sell magazines. What is a natural for AOL to sell? DSL high-speed Internet access! With DSL you can talk on the phone and have your computer on-line at the same time. Many customer service problems are hard to solve because the customer has only one phone line, which makes it hard guarantee that the problem is solved because the customer has to hang up to try it.

AOL call centers are divided into customer service teams. They compete with other teams to sell the most products in addition to meeting customer service metrics such as average customer member call time and the number of transfers to other departments.

Feet on the Street

Inside sales and telesales need a script. Outside sales needs a script and a process. Having a process enable sales to predict where a customer is with respect to making a purchasing decision. Both ACT! and Siebel's Customer Relationship Management software provide a process.

It can be as simple as:
- ❑ Customer contacted
- ❑ Needs identified
- ❑ Competition identified
- ❑ Proposal generated
- ❑ Proposal in review with client
- ❑ Proposal accepted
- ❑ Contract signed
- ❑ Contract implemented
- ❑ Contract completed
- ❑ Lessons learned captured and shared

Successful sales groups also have techniques to evaluate which Request for Proposal or Request for Quotes are worthy of response.

Value-Based Pricing

The case of airlines is one of the best examples of providing value-based pricing. Airlines and farmers both recognize the time value of a perishable product. Once a plane takes off, an empty seat is worth nothing. It is spoiled.

United Airlines has an inventory management system named Orion to maximize revenue (seat prices). They assume that vacation and leisure travelers who plan months in advance will look for bargains. The business traveler who just found out today that he has to leave tomorrow will pay through the nose. The exception is members of the Fortune 30, who have guaranteed revenue for specific airlines and as a result can get almost anywhere for about $500 at anytime.

It's not just airlines that use information technology and change the price depending upon some perceived value. Progressive Insurance Co. began as an insurer of risky drivers. They believe there are no bad risks, just bad rates. Using algorithms and extensive data, they price for profit. And just as distribution is important to Wal-Mart, the distribution of prices to 30,000 independent agents and 1,500 direct salespersons is a critical success factor for Progressive.

However, this can backfire. Coca Cola received bad press for researching soda machines that would change price as it got hotter outside. Amazon.com was caught trying out various prices on the net. E-retail will disappear if customers believe that prices are tied to their income, data that e-retailers could easily gather.

Ask yourself: Is there a value-based pricing model you should consider? When does your offering "spoil"?

Use Information Technology to Mine Data

Wal-Mart is using its checkout data to mine information about purchase patterns. This information is used to collocate similar items. Thus flashlights will be in the Outdoors Area of the store and also in the Halloween display. Bug spray will be located with the sun tan lotion and also with the camping gear. The data is also used to determine what might be a leading indicator of something they should stock. For example, when people buy Pampers, what else do they buy? Wal-Mart knows!

Ask yourself: What data does your company provide you?

Timing Is Everything

What if the customer has already purchased something and doesn't need your offering? The key is to know when it will need to be replaced. One company purchases courthouse records to gather data about a specific product that has been leased. They begin to target the customer about a year in advance of the lease expiration.

In some states you can purchase a list of cars that are registered and their owner's address. There is a wealth of information there. One car company uses this information and adds it to their trade-in data. They keep track of the trade-ins and know whom to target demographically. How much longer before a '93 Saturn with 130,000 miles is going to be replaced? One car company knows and the other four do not have a clue.

They do not have a better car, but they are better at connecting with a customer at a time when the customer would be inclined to buy. So if someone offers you free oil change and tire rotation if you test-drive one of their cars, don't take it. You may end up with thirty-six months of payments.

Ask yourself: Do you know the best window of opportunity to go back to a customer?

Usage Pricing Vs. Capacity Pricing

When Xerox Corp. introduced the first copier, it had no business model that was fair to both the light and heavy user. What is a fair monthly fee? Some people make lots of copies, while others make only a few.

They compromised and created a Usage Pricing model. A customer paid a monthly fee and one-quarter of a cent per copy.

In software, usage pricing is based on the actual use of a particular piece of software. This is different than capacity-based pricing, which is based upon the overall capacity of the hardware platform. The usage option is attractive when applications consume less than 25 percent of a system's resources.[9]

In cargo container shipping, the pricing is tied to weight and volume. Ergo, if one can fill a cargo container, volume-based pricing is preferred.

Salad bars often weigh the food to determine the price to be charged (capacity), whereas buffets more often have a fixed price (usage).

You local financial advisor probably charges a fixed 1 percent of assets no matter how often you call—if you have a $1,000,000. The rest of us are charged per visit.

For Marketing and Sales

Do you have different types of clients that should be priced differently? And, if you do, what is the potential risk?

The Customer Loyalty Grid™

When you can name a thing, you have power over it.
—Kobi James

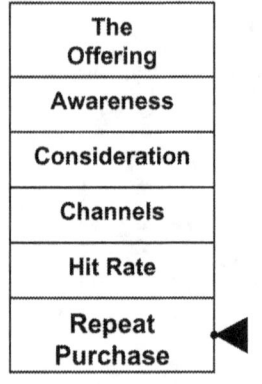

The ability to name a thing and to find the difference that makes a difference are two attributes required for business leadership and success. This is most evident when it comes to the concepts of customer loyalty, customer satisfaction, and customer retention.

Customer satisfaction is not the same as customer loyalty. A criterion of customer loyalty is customer satisfaction, but customer satisfaction in and of itself is not sufficient.

I EXPECT TO BE SATISFIED! Don't you? If customers aren't satisfied, they will not come back—unless you hold them captive.

Customers remain loyal when it is *in their best interest* to do so. Customer loyalty is not like loyalty to a sports team. Sports loyalty is emotional; customer loyalty is pragmatic. One of the reasons for lack of loyalty to sports teams is the teams' lack of loyalty to the cities and the people who paid the taxes to build stadiums.

Loyalty in business is earned by providing value. There will always be relationship buyers, but the buying process in many purchases is becoming more and more complex and requires the participation of many.

Loyalty is a function of the value you provide and the degree you are integrated into their business.

Customer Loyalty Defined™

Customer Loyalty is a function of the value a vendor provides and the degree to which a vendor is integrated into the customer's enterprise.

Value here means something the customer **perceives as beneficial**. Value changes over time. Recognizing the changes as they occur is essential to profitability.

Customer Loyalty Grid ™

High	Satisfied, but you are replaceable	Satisfied, sees you as an asset	Customer sees you as a partner
Your Value as Perceived by the Customer	Customer sees you as commodity	Satisfied, sees you as an asset	Satisfied, sees you as an asset
Low	Customer sees you as commodity	Customer sees you as necessary	Customer feels like a captive

**Degree You Are Integrated into High
the Customer's Business**

Satisfied but Replaceable

Most companies are in the upper-left-hand corner of the grid. They do most things right and are seen as valuable. However, they are vulnerable to niche players who offer a lower price.

Low-price players are sensitive to public opinion. When it was revealed that Wal-Mart was selling products manufactured overseas with child labor, the company immediately started an advertising campaign that championed its devotion to using American suppliers.

Both Wal-Mart and Costco work on slim margins and do not like returns. Returned goods are an expense that destroys profit. As a result, these retailers stop doing business with companies that cannot provide quality. This raises the bar for everyone else.

Be the Destination

Both Wal-Mart and Costco seek to be destination sites. They provide everything from shorts to soup. The Costco approach is to have unadvertised specials on things you just have to have—if you know they are on sale. Because the sales are not advertised, you have to keep coming back. Kohl's seeks to be a destination by not being in malls where customers can easily compare prices.

The Mall of America in Minnesota seeks to be a stopover for Japanese travelers crossing the United States from New York to San Francisco. It also seeks to draw in everyone from western Wisconsin to North Dakota and South Dakota. The mall has Camp Snoopy for the kids, movies and restaurants for adults, an aquarium, and enough leading national retailers to keep any shopper happy. In retail, the difference that makes a difference is to be a destination.

Clustering is another strategy. In downtown Pittsburgh, the May Company has a lock on Fifth Avenue. Its retail stores—Kaufmann's, Lord & Taylor, and Saks Fifth Avenue—sit next to Federated Department Store Inc.'s Lazarus, making the street a department store heaven.[10]

Be the Value-Added Brand

Being a value-added brand is another strategy. Who is perceived as having better quality—Sony or Panasonic? When someone is purchasing a radio, it usually is a Sony when prices are comparable. Being a value-added brand moves you from the upper-left quadrant of the Customer Loyalty Grid™ toward the center.

Bundling

Marketing uses the concept of **bundling** to group products to enhance purchases. For example, Toro uses bundling to capture sales at golf courses. It bundles lawn mowing and automatic watering in one package. The European Economic Community vetoed General Electric's purchase of Honeywell because the EEC feared GE would bundle its jet engines with Honeywell avionics.

Satisfied, Sees You as an Asset

What about all those areas in which you are seen only as an asset?

First of all, congratulate yourself. You are doing many things right.

In many ways, you become an asset in much the same way you move into being a partner. Companies use different tactics.

One common tactic is to find an important stakeholder and support it. Dell Computer Corp. supplies Web sites to its customers' support staff.

Microsoft also focuses on IT personnel, providing free seminars on upcoming releases. For end users, Microsoft provides free clip art.

Customer Loyalty Grid ™

High			
Your Value as Perceived by the Customer	Satisfied, but you are replaceable	Satisfied, sees you as an asset	Customer sees you as a partner
	Customer sees you as commodity	Satisfied, sees you as an asset	Satisfied, sees you as an asset
Low	Customer sees you as commodity	Customer sees you as necessary	Customer feels like a captive

Degree You Are Integrated into **High**
the Customer's Business

American Express quantifies the value of its card to retail clients by explicitly pointing out how much revenue the client gained by accepting the American Express card from its customers.

Companies seen as assets, more often than not, provide newsletters that contain useful information. Many non-asset companies provide newsletters that are "light" or "fluff" and contain little solid information. These newsletters are used to create Awareness and to keep their name in front of a client.

Newsletters from companies seen as assets are often sent by e-mail with links to additional information. One indicator of the value of the newsletter is whether past editions are available on-line and how often they are accessed.

Customer Service: Best Practice Tip

Did you know that the difference that makes a difference in customer satisfaction is asking:
"Are you 100 percent satisfied?"
Followed by, "What did you like best?"
By asking these questions, you learn what was special to the customers. You also find out if you need to correct any shortfalls.

Using this technique, you create advocates for your offering. You end up with customers telling their friends about your good work and why they liked you! You have helped your customers create a story they will tell their friends and associates.

Customer Sees You as a Partner

How does one get into the upper-right corner of the Loyalty Grid? Whether you are creating a new offering or providing a service, how do you make yourself perceived as the most desirable choice? You have to be involved in the customer's business. You need to provide a solution.

There are several approaches:

- ❑ IBM adopted a strategy of moving away from selling boxes to being trusted **advisors**.
- ❑ SAP and Lawson Software provide an enterprise software **system**, as opposed to an application.
- ❑ Manufacturers sell *services* to become involved in the customer's business. General Electric Corp. will service an airline's jet engines. IBM will run your Web site. Intel will provide you with a server farm. Xerox will run your reproduction center. AT&T will run your network.

What about Microsoft? Do companies feel like Microsoft has their best interests at heart? We hear of IBM recommending competitors' products. Would Microsoft do that?

The difference that makes a difference is to answer one question: Do you really have the client's best interest at heart? This attitude is exemplified in *Miracle on 34th Street* when the Macy's Santa Claus sent customers to Gimbels. Being perceived as having that attitude means you are seen as a partner.

Being a partner enables you to work even more closely with your customers than you do now. This is easier to say than do, especially if you do not have a broad array of offerings. This is when alliances with other companies come into play. When you form an alliance with other companies to provide a solution, your customers will perceive you as having greater value.

The alternative to alliances is to expand your services to meets clients' needs. Ingram Micro, an electronics distributor, provides specialists to help the Value-Added Resellers it supports. A bank in Minnesota advertises that it provides a team of specialists to small-and medium-sized businesses. The bank can meet all the business clients' needs.

Be Consistent

It is difficult to consistently have the best interests of the customer at heart, especially when your company has a large number of persons who come into contact with customers. Appropriate policy should be well understood by personnel who come into contact with the customer. The policy should have the best interest of the customer in mind.

One road warrior began to fly American Airlines rather than Northwest. When asked why, she said, "Our Friday meeting ended at 11 a.m., so I got to the airport early, about 12:20, on the hotel shuttle. There was a flight at 2 p.m. in addition to my full 5 p.m. flight. The two o'clock flight was only half full, but because of my ticket, Northwest wanted to charge me an additional $300! I couldn't see asking the company to pay for that, so I took the five o'clock flight and got home at midnight."

Technically the Northwest counter representative did the right thing. But it was short-sighted. Northwest not only lost the customer's repeat business but also lost the opportunity to make a last-minute walk-up of a stand-by passenger able to catch the 5 p.m. flight.

Customer Retention Is Not Customer Loyalty

Customers usually are not loyal to an airline; they are loyal to frequent flyer miles. When companies prohibit employees from banking frequent flyer miles, they find that employees are taking cheaper flights and staying at less expensive hotels. We all want to have repeat business, but we need to recognize if it is due to the value you provide or the bonus points you provide. Others can copy award programs, but value is hard to copy.

Retention Is a Good Thing (Loyalty Is Better)

It is true that both customer retention and employee retention strategies work. One hears comments such as:

"I only have one more year until I am vested, so I won't quit until then."

"I stay at Marriott because I get free nights."

"I always fly ___ because they upgrade me to first class."

Notice how they have their personal best interests at heart.

Example: AT&T WorldNet Service Retention Program

AT&T WorldNet is an Internet Service Provider. Its retention program rewards members with free software as a thank-you for continuing membership. AT&T WorldNet Service members are able to participate in the program after they have used the service for four consecutive months. At that time, members receive an e-mail informing them of their eligibility in the AT&T WorldNet Service Software Rewards program. After four months, a member can choose from ten software titles; after eight months, twenty titles; and after twelve months, fifty titles. This approach rewards customers who remain longer.

Training as a Sales Competitive Advantage

How is it that at Circuit City the inside salespersons can answer so many questions? It is no accident. Circuit City has high-speed Internet access providing streaming video on technologies, products, and features.

Many a sales and marketing manager have missed using training as a competitive advantage. Training managers often can have substantial influence on the launch of a new offering. In one example, a sales training manager went the extra mile and researched the requirements of the channel in addition to the requirements he was given for the product launch for the direct sales force. The product introduction was an overwhelming success because channel sales were triple those predicted. The channels saw the manufacturer as a partner, not just a provider.

Don't dismiss staff training. Workers at Target, the discount store, dust the top shelves, even though no one can see them. Target stores are cleaner than Wal-Mart and K-Mart stores because of training and management controls. Five will get you ten you will see dusty television sets at Target's competitors.

Business Architectures to Block the Competition

How are you growing? Is it like the old farmhouse with one room added after another or is there a master plan?

Business Architectures involve the strategies of how a company goes to the marketplace. Being aware of these approaches facilitates blocking the competition.

How does one create a barrier that will keep the competition away from your customers? It has to do with price versus actual and perceived value, barriers to entry, and customer satisfaction.

In a service economy the key to customer satisfaction is quality service at every Moment of Truth. A Moment of Truth occurs whenever a customer comes into contact with your personnel or entity, such as the Web site.

The Customer Loyalty Grid™ helps you understand where you stand from the Customer's Point of View.

Now we will look at the foundations or architectures you need to install to keep the competition at bay.

What is Foundation Architecture?

When information technology personnel think of architecture, they think in terms of mainframes or client servers. They decide if they are an Oracle shop or IBM database shop. The power of choosing architecture is that skills can be concentrated in a vital few areas. If employees were allowed to have any software and hardware they choose, there would be compatibility problems.

Construction personnel understand architectures. If a concrete floor is poured a certain way it can only support offices; manufacturing floors are more expensive because they must to support the heavy equipment.

So what are the architectures or strategies to block the competition?

The Chain-Link Fence

This is a strategy used when you have a patentable offering. Patents often cover a specific formulation or arrangement.

Competitors will use a Design of Experiments Analysis, such as Taguchi's approach, and patent viable options.

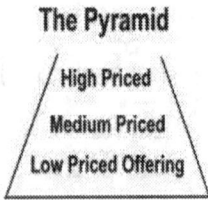

Imagine that the center of the fence is the area of viable offerings based upon the chemistry and physics of offering. As shown in the sketch, when all the viable options are locked up, it is like a chain-link fence. You can see through to the customers, but you cannot create an offering that is viable because none exists. Japanese companies are excellent at using Design of Experimentation to identify viable formulations. Then they patent them.

The Pyramid

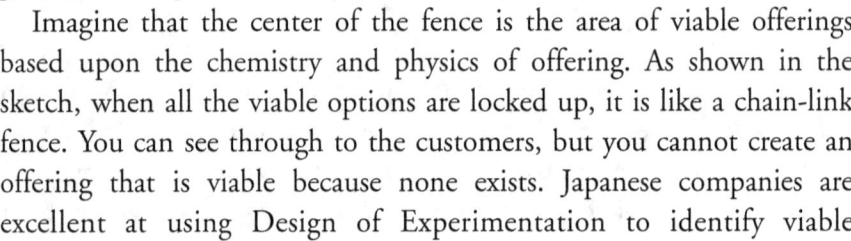

The pyramid structure is often used where there are price points that provide openings for the competition.

Perrier provides a classic example of this technique. Perrier buys up local water companies maintaining local supermarket shelf space and often being a low-price entry. However, if customers want a Premium-Priced product, the supermarket will also stock Perrier.

Be the solution

Do you want a fully integrated operating system with applications that exchange data? Try Microsoft.

Do you want to install a fully integrated enterprise-wide system that works across various platforms? Try IBM.

Solutions can fill niches like Siebel's Customer Relationship Management software or be comprehensive like a turnkey warehouse.

In the childhood game Scissors Paper Stone, Paper bests Stone by wrapping it. Solutions wrap products.

Centrally Decentralize

In the sixties, IBM had manufacturing plants throughout Europe. However, no one country had enough of its manufacturing to nationalize the computer company. In other words, expertise was decentralized.

Today, the same idea is being used in Modular Manufacturing. Different vendors provide complete assemblies. While they may gain an expertise in one area, they never make the entire offering. At one location all the assemblies come together to be joined into the final offering. What are the benefits?

- ❑ The "manufacturer" has less inventory and can take advantage of the skill sets of the suppliers.
- ❑ Just as in the human body, where there are specialized cells for hearing and seeing and digesting foods, there are manufacturing cells that specialize in their applications.

Standard Interfaces

The Lego® block model enables a child to create a fort or a bridge because of the standard interface. Microsoft gave us the Windows operating system, enabling IBM PC clones. Similarly, bar codes enable everyone to keep track of materials easier.

When the standard interface becomes ubiquitous, it becomes the standard that others must follow. Thus the World Wide Web Consortium develops Internet Protocols, or IPs, that everyone follows.

Quality and Branding Have Changed the Competitive Landscape

Quality standards enable discount prices. There was a time in the seventies that low-price retailers sold lower-quality goods. The baby boomers, those born between 1946 and 1964, were brought up with the idea that low price meant low quality. K-Mart products did not last as long as Saks Fifth Avenue or the local department store. Sears and J.C. Penney stores provided quality for Middle America.

Being a Brand meant a promise of quality. The eighties eroded some brands. Automobile tires are now imprinted with how long they will last, regardless of the manufacturer.

One reason Wal-Mart has grown is the spread of the quality movement. It is the quality movement of the nineties that contributed to Wal-Mart's success. Mass-produced brands from Procter and Gamble or Perdue Chickens strive to be on Wal-Mart's shelves.

Today K-Mart carries the brands of Martha Stewart linens and Kathy Ireland clothes. Brands like these used to be found only in department stores.

What is that brand that Linens and Things or Bed, Bath and Beyond carry? If you cannot answer that question, you should not buy their stock.

For Marketing and Sales

If you cannot create standard interfaces, become the standard (i.e., Oracle for e-commerce).

If you cannot become the standard, be ubiquitous (i.e., Windows operating system on PCs).

If you cannot create a de facto standard by being ubiquitous, become the Original Equipment Manufacturer/Original Service Provider (i.e., Whirlpool making Sears' Kenmore washing machines).

If you cannot be the OEM/OSP, partner with many others (i.e., Microsoft providing software for over twenty manufacturers of Personal Digital Assistants).

If you cannot be the OEM, give it away for free and charge for the training or the supplies. When you become the standard, you can charge for the offering, the "new, improved version," or maintenance. Red Hat didn't invent Linux; it provides Linux training and software.

Always maintain quality and build brand.

Customer Use Cycle™

Business is simple; you just have to think like a customer.
—Kobi James

Is there a tool that Sales and Marketing can use to increase value during the customer's shopping experience? To alter their consideration or increase repeat purchases? There is—it is called the Customer Use Cycle™.

First the Customer Needs to Understand the Benefit

The Customer Use Cycle™ (CUC) is customer-centric, meaning that it focuses on the Need through Replacement Process from the Customer's Point of View (POV). It supports the Tsunami Process in four major areas as indicated at the left.

Often there are services or features that we provide for a customer that they fail to appreciate unless we **explain the benefit** to them. Listed below are some examples of benefits that were not immediately obvious to the customer:

One computer has a 56K modem built in, while the other does not, yet they are the same price. The purchaser was not aware that to be connected to the Internet would require the purchase of a modem.

One manufacturer of PC chips supplies a cache (useful for holding Web pages when surfing the net); the other does not.

One refrigerator has an energy saver feature that only costs $25 extra and can help reduce energy needs during vacations. It will pay for itself many times over, if the customer knows its true value.

One training company keeps records of CEUs (Continuing Education Units) units for seven years. This can be of great benefit to students who need a record of their training.

One company has free delivery and removes the old product. The department store also has free delivery, but charged $35 to remove the old product.

The Customer Use Cycle™ assumes a knowledgeable customer, one that has had time to go onto the Internet, review Gardner Reports, check out *Consumer Reports,* or speak to their friends. It also assumes **you are identifying the offerings benefits** from the customer's point of view. Customers do not care about a feature or attribute if they do not understand the benefit they receive from the feature.

The CUC looks at the total life cycle a customer goes through to identify, obtain, use, and replace an offering. It is used to obtain competitive advantage.

Customer Use Cycle™

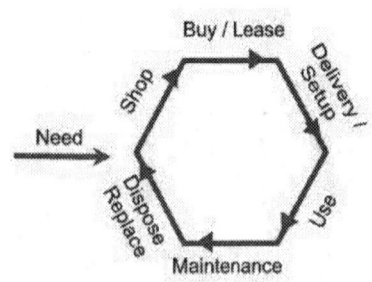

Companies win contracts, clients, and market share by strengthening their advantage in areas the customer values. These areas, as shown on the diagram, start with identifying the Needs of the Customer. Here you Create Awareness, Consideration, and work towards Demand Creation.

In Shopping you need to be convenient. Your sales staff needs to be expert in how to position your offering. Are there ways to finance the offering?

How easy is it to obtain the offering? How does the customer get it to their place of business or home?

Do you provide help in Using it or in Maintenance?

What is involved in Disposing of (replacing or upgrading) your offering? Do you replace yourself or does your competition replace you?

An example of each of these areas follows.

Clarifying Need

❑ At Burnsville Hitch, they only install hitches and educate the customers as to the correct Class 1 or Class 2 hitch they need for towing. Because this is their niche, they can install a hitch in twenty minutes at a price that is 30 percent less than their competition.

❑ Office Depot asks their clients which applications they want to run on their PCs and then makes a recommendation for a suitable computer.

- ❑ Gateway stores show computer displays for making music CDs or surfing the net.
- ❑ A local dentist sends out post cards reminding patients it is time for another checkup.
- ❑ Saturn includes a $5 off coupon with their reminder of the need for an oil change.

Shopping

- ❑ Need a new nose? One Hollywood plastic surgeon **shows you** what your face will look like using a computer image.
- ❑ Amazon.com has over 100,000 Web site partners. When you are at a partner site and decide to purchase a product, you often can click on an "order now" button and be taken directly to the Amazon.com Web site. Partners get up to a 15 percent referral fee. Customers are provided **an easy** way to get what they want.

Buy/Lease

- ❑ The Ford Web site can **help you decide** if buying or leasing is better for you.
- ❑ The Home Shopping Network spreads out the cost of a $90 piece of jewelry over two payments. **Spreading out the payments** makes it easier for customers.
- ❑ Lucent and Cisco loaned money to startups if they used their equipment. (Yes, there were problems when the dot-com crash occurred.)

Delivery and Setup (Configuration)

- ❑ A bank in England wanted 2,700 Pentium II PCs and 800 servers. IBM dropped out of the bidding because they could not match the HP and Dell prices. The HP and Dell bids were nearly identical except for one thing. The HP reseller would only ship the order to the bank's headquarters, whereas Dell would **deliver ready-to-boot machines to each of the bank's 450 branches at no added cost.** The bank estimates it saved $750,000.[11]
- ❑ A manufacturer of self-assemble bookcases **redesigned** them so that even if they were put together backwards, the bookcase still came out correct.

- ❏ Office Depot offers **free delivery** to your home or place of business on orders of $50 or more.
- ❏ Media Cybernetics, a software provider, began providing the hardware as well as the software, thus creating a **total solution** for the customer, and turned the company around.

Use

- ❏ Some software comes with wizards, a **pre-programmed set of directions** that leads you through common tasks.
- ❏ Microsoft provides ninety days **free phone support** when you purchase MS Office.
- ❏ Dell Computer has created Premier pages for 4,000 companies' customized Web portals. Dell focuses on supplying **help to the clients' in-service help desks** to make the clients' internal support more efficient.

Maintain

- ❏ Xerox Corp. **will train customers** to perform simple maintenance on Xerox printers.
- ❏ Large Xerox copiers have **sensors that can predict** when a copier will have a problem and **call in for service.**
- ❏ A Latrobe, PA doctor gives **free medication** to his clients. These come from the sample packs left by the pharmaceutical sales reps, saving his poorer patients money.

Dispose/Replace (or Transfer Data)

- ❏ Xerox will upgrade your printer and take away the old one.
- ❏ A tire company does not charge to dispose of the old tires.
- ❏ The local food store has a bin for recycling phone books. Customers can shop after they drop off their books.

For Marketing and Sales Managers

Think about the **totality of the experience** from the customer's point of view. The offering in and of itself may not be of sufficient value without all the support that surrounds it.

Following is a checklist of the most common options businesses are using today.

What Can You Do to Help the Customer?

		Note
Need	• Educate client • Promote your approach • Prepare Request for Proposal • Develop proofs of benefits	
Shop	• Demos • Test product • Trial period • CD-ROM, videos • Visits to (resort, factory, etc.) • Computer simulations	
Buy or Lease	• Terms and conditions • Break up payments • Automatic (e) deductions • Provide financing • Volume discounts • Interest-free period	
Arrange delivery and setup	• Assistance • Tracking of material • Expediters • Easy to do (fail safe)	
Use	• Training • Design for ease of use • Ergonomic factors • Ease of ordering supplies • Guarantees • Warning indicators	
Maintain	• Service contracts • Free upgrades • Reliability • Replace what fails • Up time guarantee • 1-800 service numbers in US • Service level agreements	
Dispose / Replace	• Replace • Upgrade • Recycle	

An Example of Success through Providing a Solution[12]

Media Cybernetics LP in Maryland, USA, produces image analysis software products. The software is used to reduce cycle times and inspections by retrieving and analyzing images for compliance with ISO 9000 or government regulations. The sales model ignored the customer's need to obtain the hardware necessary to use the software. By creating a solution sales model, in which the software product was combined with components and services, the annual growth became 30-plus percent. Michael Galvin, CEO of Media Cybernetics LP, also recommended the following tactics in an interview with *Nations Business:*

Form Alliances

He formed distribution alliances so that the whole solution would arrive easily, be installed easily, and be set up for use.

Increase Your Dealer and User Training

Galvin trained dealers how to sell the solution to customers based upon their needs. Together with dealers they trained customers how to better use the products.

Ensure Partners Commit to Leadership in Price and Performance

This way partners continually improve and upgrade their offerings.

Partner with OEMs

Letting original equipment manufacturers use their own private labels opened new channels not covered by his dealers.

Somerset Custom Houseboats:
An Example of Getting Involved With the Customer

At Somerset Custom Houseboats, a customer can visit the Web site and see photos of their $250,000-boat being built. They believe they sell a lifestyle, not a boat. Part of the lifestyle includes sponsoring regattas. They borrowed the idea from Harley Davidson. To make it easier to obtain their product, they even provide boat insurance. (On the Customer Loyalty Grid™ what quadrant might they be in?)

Perhaps you sell through distributors or resellers. The approach is the same. Identify what they want.

What Do Distributors, Resellers, and Value-Added Resellers Want?

If an indirect channel were your customer, ask yourself what you would want if you were their shoes. How do they decide to sell your offering or your competitor's?

Benchmarking is a common tool used to compare service or product features.

An example of a vendor checklist to determine whom they partner with follows.

How Your Channels Rate You

Criteria	You	Competitor
PROFIT		
Maximum Profit as Margin		
Minimum Quantity Discounts		
Sales Collaterals		
Incentives (buy Z get X free)		
SALES		
More / sales leads		
Sales referrals		
Dedicated sales representative		
Team selling		
FIELD SUPPORT		
Conflict Resolution		
Meetings with customers		
Developing Proposals		
Developing beta proof of concept		

Technical support fees
   Per call
   Flat fee		

Joint seminars		
Joint training		
Trade shows		
RETURNS (OF PRODUCT)		
Who owns the customer?		
How much advance notice is provided when changes occur?		
How is inventory handled?		

Are you the best choice?

For Marketing and Sales

Sales and Marketing need to stay focused on tracking how the competition provides value in the customer's shopping experience. Sales touch the customer and needs to answer the question, "What was the difference that made the difference in selecting us for the vendor?"

Marketing needs to create the infrastructure to make the shopping experience more efficient and pleasant, as compared to the competition from the customer's point of view.

Putting It Together

When ants travel they leave an invisible odor on the ground. When they find a food source they go back to the colony having left a trail to the food. As more ants follow the trail to the food, the trail gets stronger, thus reinforcing the route. In systems theory this is called a reinforcing loop.

The following figure shows where the models have the greatest impact on the Tsunami Model™. The Kano Model reinforces the Tsunami Process because Kano identifies the features and attributes desired by the end users, whether they be our channels of the end users or our offerings. The Customer Use Cycle helps us differentiate ourselves in the customers' eyes. It impacts the Offering, Consideration, the Hit Rate, and Repeat Purchases. We become more desirable to our customers. The following figure shows where the models have the greatest impact on the Tsunami Model™.

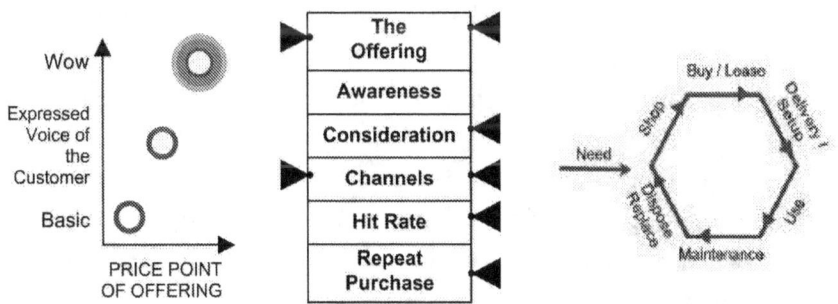

The more we use the models and leave a written trail behind for others to understand what we have done, the stronger we become as a company. We begin to develop competencies that become competitive strengths.

General Electric Corp. is an example of building strengths and capacities that support the customer. GE had gotten into services because of their higher profit margin. When Wal-Mart announced that it was going to sell appliances it also announced that it was partnering

61

with GE. GE had the product, and more importantly, it also had the capacity for service and delivery. Wal-Mart had storefronts and millions of customer visits but lacked delivery.

There are many other examples. Ingram Micro is a distributor of electronic equipment. They supply Value-Added Resellers with the hardware and computers so that businesses can have networks. Ingram Micro also supplies technical advice. They are such a good distributor that they are the e-supplier for the Amazon.com and Best Buy on-line computer outlets.

The Easiest Way to Increase Profits

What is the easiest way to increase profits? Increase prices. Some industries do it automatically. Pharmaceuticals often have annual increases every January. But Brystol-Myers raised its diabetic drug, Glucophage, 8 percent in January 2001 and 4.9 percent in May, for a total of almost 13 percent. Schering-Plough raised the price of its allergy medicine, the purple pill Claritin, four times in 2000 and also in 2001.[13]

How does one increase prices? Raise your prices to almost match the competition.

Penske Auto Repair increased the labor costs to replace car struts almost 100 percent from June 2001 to December 2001.

Wal-Mart is the "low cost leader." They are not always the lowest cost. Prices depend upon local competitive environments.

GM was reported considering charging extra for safety features, such as side air bags. (They haven't yet.)

In many areas DSL service has increased from $39 to $59 monthly.

How do auto companies raise prices? Monthly, if the car is popular. Or they will give a rebate and then increase prices over the next few months. To keep prices down, the automobile companies have been aggressive with their suppliers. It is assumed that a component that cost $1 this year will cost 93 cents next year due to process improvements and Six Sigma.

Date	Sticker Price	Destination Charge	Rebate	Impact Over Previous Month
2002 Ford Escape XLT				
March 2002	$22,395	$540	$0	
April 2002	$23,830 (up 435)	$565 (up 15)	$500 (up 500)	$50 saving
2002 Chrysler Town and Country LX Minivan				
Feb. 2002	$25,015 (up 135)	$655	$2500	Up $135
March 2002	$25,165 (up 150)	$680 (up 25)	$2500	Up $157

Source: White, Gregory L and Lundergaard, Karen. Sticker Shock. *The Wall Street Journal* 10 April 2002 Page D1.

To increase prices, first you have to consider your competitive environment. If you do not know what your competition is charging, you do not know what the local market will support. One company we worked with discovered that they were charging less than half of their competition's price. Originally they had been concerned that they might lose customers if they increased prices 4 percent!

It is no small task to understand the competition. Large Fortune 100 companies have programs with databases of regional labor rates, raw material costs, energy costs, and shipping rates. They can accurately predict the cost to provide a product or service in fifty countries.

Sometimes there are complications when you add value that your competition does not provide. For example, what should you charge for a four-in-one printer-copier-scanner-fax machine? Should you charge as much as you would for four individual machines? If one breaks down will all functions cease? (The Internet was designed with seven protocol levels, which is why one application may fail yet you can still use another, such as e-mail.)

Of course if you do have a multifunctional device, all the functions are lost when the device goes into the repair shop.

The answer on how much to charge is "it depends." Asian-based companies often look at **what a customer will pay** and then subtract the **cost to produce and deliver the offering**. The difference is the profit. European-and American-based companies look at the **cost to produce and deliver**, add on a **profit,** and the combination is the price to the consumer.

There are price point clusters. These exist because of the perceived value of the offering and the availability of substitute offerings. Thus DVD players slowly sold at $400, mainly to Early Adopters. Potential customers already had video cassette players. However, at $120 DVD players sold like hotcakes. Broadband does not sell at $55 per month or $660 per year, but at an introductory price of $20 per month for three months, it is cheaper than Internet Service Providers such as AOL or MSN. The hope is that after three months the customer will be hooked on the speed of the service.

Secondly, you have to decide whether on not to charge for a feature. This is done by considering the cost to produce it and the value the feature provides to your customers. The "Cost to Produce versus Value to the Seller" that follows provides guidance.

Cost to Produce versus Value to Buyer

Cost to Seller	High	Delete feature	Charge	Charge extra
		"Why do we	Charge	Charge
	Low	offer this feature?"	Offer Free	Charge or Offer Free
		Low		High

Value to Buyer

High Cost, Low Value

If the cost to produce a feature is high, perhaps you should get rid of it if there is not market segment that truly wants it. The more it costs to produce a feature, the more it should be accounted into the price of the offering. This is true even for a service. For example, do you charge for travel time to get to the next customer or do you include travel time as part of the overall cost?

Low Cost, High Value

If the cost to produce a highly valued feature is low, you could provide it for free to encourage good will. If your competition does not provide it, you could charge extra. Since it costs little to produce, it will increase your margins.

Defeaturing, Downsizing

This brings us to the last lesson of this chapter. Defeaturing enables you to provide an offering at a lower price point. Using standard interfaces and standard components on a platform enables Marketing and Sales to have a Product Family. It is easier to focus on the customer when you have a family of offerings at different price points.

Some Japanese companies will include all the features on an electronic product; however, the features are obscured by the cover or defeated by a jumper cable. When a component is spread out over a larger product run, its incremental cost drops. Yes, the profit is less on one model, but there is an advantage to being able to quickly switch models.

This is called the product family Total Cost of Production. The reduced work involved in production, configuration control, and quality control can save manufacturers 5 percent. Thus a Canon copier may have a paper-sizing sensor on all four models of a product family, but it is only activated on the two higher-priced models.

Companies will also downsize their offering when energy or component costs increase.

Candy companies reduce the weight of the candy when sugar prices go up. The packaging and the price remain the same.

At Bed, Bath and Beyond, their corner shelving unit shrunk by two inches while the price remained the same. The unit shrunk four shelves and one wooden post is no longer used.

One consulting company reduced its price but added on travel costs. Travel had been included at the previous price.

This book you are reading is the "Readers Digest" version of the CD-ROM.

Top Four Lists

Together we are smarter than any one of us.

One person who reviewed the book said, "This is all very interesting, but is there anything you can give me that would help my team improve sales? I don't have the authority to do this stuff."

"Sure," I replied.

A best practice is to generate Top Four lists. Top Four lists provide options to situations and problems.

For example, what are the top fours ways to overcome a client's sticker shock? What are the top four ways to reply when the prospect mentions Competitor's X's feature? What are the top four ways to handle an unethical request?

Companies that have top four lists make more money. They are becoming a Learning Organization. This is tough in sales because often it is very competitive.

The process is simple, ask a question and then brainstorm some answers. Pick the top four. For example, what are the top four ways to generate referrals from current clients?

First, let's make an assumption: It is easy to get referrals. If you do a good job, and if your customer is satisfied, why wouldn't he or she say nice things about you? Wouldn't you let yourself be used as a reference if someone did a good job for you?

Here are the top four approaches from a Singapore sales team.

1. Ask for external referrals: Whenever you have been successful in satisfying a client's needs, ask the client if he or she knows someone you could help **and** ask if you could use the client's name.

2. Ask for internal referrals: Many companies are broken into lines of business and your client could be one of five or more buyers in the same company.

3. 80-20 Rule: Often 80 percent of your profits come from 20 percent of your clients. Treat them very well and ask who they see as their equivalent at other companies. Your customers belong to networks and professional societies.

4. Reward your clients: One sales representative in Minnesota takes her six biggest clients on a fishing trip. Another provides dinner for two at an upscale restaurant for

successful leads. This creates indebtedness and they are more likely to give you referrals.

5. Provide incentives: Send an incentive letter to clients offering them the opportunity to be in a drawing for a car first aid/emergency kit. It doesn't matter if the referrals work out or not. For the referrals that do work out, provide that client's office free bagels, donuts, and coffee for a month of Fridays. Provide a book of ten movie or video rental passes, or a trip to the spa, or—well you get the idea.

6. Get your client clients: Do you look for opportunities to recommend your client to others? Referrals lead to referrals. It is called quid pro quo.

7. Treat your clients like human beings: Harvey MacKay, in his book *Swim with the Sharks Without Being Eaten Alive,* lists sixty-eight data points you should know about your clients. Send them birthday cards, anniversary cards, and copies of articles that would help them in their business. They will give you referrals.

8. Ask for a written testimonial: Many training companies ask if they can print their clients' comments from the evaluation sheets.

9. Help them present to a local professional society or Chamber of Commerce: If your offering saved them money or improved ROI, help them have a higher standing with their fellow professionals. Networking is important in this economy. Naturally you will be there for the presentation.

10. Reduce the cost of doing business: Offer the same for less. They will love you.

"So there are four ideas," I said.

"Four? It looks like ten!" he replied.

"This is an example of the concept 'under promise and over deliver.'"

He grinned at me.

"Are you satisfied?" I asked.

He didn't answer my question. Instead he replied, "Let me guess, the next thing you are going to ask me is what did I like best?"

We both smiled and I asked, "And what did you like best?" I wanted to turn this client into a fan.

Appendix A:
Best Practices to Improve Profits

When looking over this list remember to use creative innovation and borrow the ideas from one business area and apply them to yours.

Alliances

Alliances can be used to increase market penetration, obtain strengths one does not have, obtain niche features, and reduce unnecessary burdens.

Smart Bombing

Many manufacturers try to find a single site that can support a large territory. Using this approach, Whirlpool could not cost justify building one plant in the Pacific. General Electric forms alliances with manufacturers overseas that will agree to quality standards and profit goals. GE called this approach Smart Bombing, utilizing local manufacturers in specific countries.

"In the summer of 1999, IBM decided against pursuing the application-software business inside the company." Why? They determined it was fragmented and moved quickly. They decided to provide middleware such as DB2 and WebSphere but not compete with CRM vendors. Thus if Siebel were to license a new CRM product, "opportunities abound in hardware and services for IBM."[14]

Northwest Airlines 1998

Northwest CEO John Dasburg reported that "We were at a strategic disadvantage to United, American, and perhaps Delta," to a University of St. Thomas Alumni Club meeting February 6, 1998.

He believed that his customer base demanded a global presence, and having hubs in major metropolitan areas gave Northwest an advantage when negotiating partnerships with foreign carriers.

Thus Northwest's winning $519-million bid for a controlling interest in Houston-based Continental Airlines. Northwest has an alliance with KLM Royal Dutch Airlines and KLM has an alliance with Alitalia, Italy's largest carrier. "Milano is probably the best future southern European hub," stated Dasburg.

Compaq in 1998

The new trend in 1998 was PC makers forging arrangements with on-line services. PC makers have redesigned their keyboards to add "quick access" to Internet features. Compaq's 1998 PCs will have four Internet buttons with automatic links to Amazon.com, Walt Disney's on-line store and America Online. If you purchase something from the on-line store, Compaq will get a fee. AOL paid a fee for the installation of the AOL button and software.

Xilinx with IBM in 2002

Xilinx, a fabless semiconductor company, announced in March 2002 the signing of a two-year, $100-million agreement under which IBM Microelectronics will manufacture critical Xilinx products.

Sandeep Vij, Xilinx's vice-president for worldwide marketing said that this deal represents the first time IBM has agreed to manufacture high-volume parts for an outside customer (This increases fixed asset utilization). IBM will be obtaining technology from Xilinx's Programmable Logic Device. Combining their technologies will result in a "system on a chip."

Kellogg's and Disney 2002

Disney was pinched by lower attendance at its theme parks. Kellogg's had sluggish sales. Disney suggested the license agreement that would put Mickey Mouse, Buzz Lightyear from *Toy Story*, and other characters on Kellogg's products. The awareness campaign shows a small child in the back seat of a car magically making things happen, such as a turning the traffic light green and opening the garage door. The tag line comes at the end: "feed their imagination."

Annuity Stream

Whenever possible, create an annuity stream. Speakers have books and tapes, but that is for additional revenue. Annuity streams come from things people buy and re-buy.

Public utilities create annuity streams. Insurance companies create annuity streams.

Credit card issuers create annuity streams. Most people pay interest.

Be a high value specialty publishers like BNA and Law Reviews.

Newsletters can be annuity streams.

Owning the right to ____ (e.g.15 million prescription refills) is an annuity stream.

Approaches

What is your company's approach or strategy in the marketplace?

IBM Business Strategy

IBM sold mainframe boxes (1980–92) and retained earnings dropped. Layoffs ensued because the marketplace was moving to distributed systems and PCs. These were the same people who missed owning a chunk of Intel and Microsoft. In 1993 IBM became a "Technology Services Company" and the turnaround has been dramatic. A *service* company's attitude is very different from a "we sell boxes" attitude.

Wal-Mart Ad Strategy

Using a commercial that shows large price signs with the pennies, dimes, and dollar values falling, Wal-Mart promotes their low-cost image. They create a perception in the customers' mind of being low cost and that prices are dropping 25 percent. In reality they take a category such as prescriptions, benchmark the most common one hundred and offer them at a lower price than the competition. Customers of the most common brands conclude they are the lowest for everything. The end result is the urban myth that Wal-Mart has the lowest prices on everything.

Office Depot

In 2002 Office Depot promoted itself as the office expert. Want information on a PDA or printer? "We are knowledgeable."

Awareness—Clever Examples

Federal Express got great billing in the Tom Hank's movie *Cast Away*. So did Wilson volleyballs.

For three months in 2002, Revlon will be featured on the ABC soap opera *All My Children*. Susan Lucci's character, Erica Kane, must battle the corporate giant as it attempts to recruit an executive from Erica's cosmetic company. "She battled kidnappers, survived a grizzly bear, overcame backstabbing in-laws and nine marriages—can she survive this new challenge?—Stay tuned!'

Awareness—Creating Awareness for Movies

Movie studios create awareness through movie trailers, sneak previews, which are now announced in advance (it used to be you did not know what you were going to see), timing exclusive articles of the actors in trade magazines, newspaper and broadcast advertising. Actors will appear on Rosie and with Jay Leno to hype the movie the week of its release. For wide release movies the television broadcast advertising ends with a clear announcement of the premier date.

Promoting a sequel on its television debut is one Awareness strategy used by the movie studios. When a James Bond movie was first shown on one of the three major networks, during the commercials there would be a plug for the upcoming release.

Sequels are timed so that they can be advertised when the first release occurs. Movie trailers often preannounce movies. Reputation has it that James Bond trailers are released to theatres as soon as the first action sequence is filmed, often a year in advance. Trailers for *102 Dalmatians* appeared on Thanksgiving 1999 for a release a year later. Song videos on MTV and VH1 add to the Awareness campaign.

Some films are seen at film expos such as the Sundance Film Festival. These may be seeking distributors.

Film critics preview almost all films so that there will be favorable opening day reviews. How are movies previewed?

❑ By video: Videos are sent to movie critics to reduce the cost of promotion.
❑ Private media showing: On a weekday, movie critics and columnists who might be influenced to write a favorable article or mention it on the evening news are invited to a private showing.

How do individuals get to see previews?

❑ By Invitation: These are held in the evening or early Saturday. Often the ten o'clock Saturday morning previews are for movies targeted at children. The seven o'clock evening showing is targeted at adults.
❑ By chance: By listening to a radio station and being the "lucky seventh caller."

Awareness—Creating Demand for a New Product

John Barden is the founder of Pumpkin Masters, a Denver, Colorado small business. His firm sells a pumpkin carving kit used at Halloween. He found that it was hard to sell an outline that could be put onto a pumpkin when many felt they could just use a kitchen knife and retailers did not have a category for the product. In 1986 they sold 50,000 kits and were in debt when a volunteer stepped forward.

Listen to the customer

She was a purchaser of Pumpkin Masters products and suggested having carvings of the ABC-TV announcers on the Halloween night football game between the Denver Broncos and the Indiana Colts. The pumpkins were shown during the game along with a scary, Barden-carved pumpkin face named "skull." It was just the impetus Pumpkin Masters needed, and in 1997 they sold 2 million kits.[15]

Awareness—Digital Signage and CBS

A digitally created CBS logo was used to block out an NBC sign in Times Square during the CBS news coverage of the New Year's Eve celebrations in 1999. The network has regularly put their image where it does not exist during the broadcast of the *The Early Show*. A CBS official called it digital signage and said, "Any time there is a NBC logo we will block it."[16]

When the trailers for the movie *Spider Man* came out in 2002, the Samsung billboard in Times Square, New York was digitally replaced with a *USA Today* newspaper plug. Samsung got the owner of the billboard to sue Sony Corp., the owner of the movie and a competitor of Samsung, for digital piracy. Samsung got its sign back in the movie.[17]

Awareness Mistakes

Toyota

In 1998, Toyota ran a print ad in *Jet Magazine*, a publication targeted at black Americans, with a caption that read, "Unlike your last boyfriend, the Corolla goes to work every morning."

In 2001, part of the RAV4 sport utility vehicle ad campaign included the distribution of free postcards at trendy clubs. One showed a dark-skinned man's mouth with the image of a gold RAV4 on one tooth. Toyota defended the ad as trendy, using the hot concept of tooth art. The Reverend Jesse Jackson thought it was racist. The ad was pulled in May.

Sony

Sony's Columbia Pictures created a fake critic, David Manning, to praise its movies in newspaper ads over a nine-month period from late 2000 through 2001. They agreed to stop the practice. However, the practice of supplying employees to pose as moviegoers in "person on the street" interviews for TV commercials may continue. Both Columbia and Fox Searchlight admitted to using that practice.

Phillip Morris

On the Monday ABC Evening News (July 16, 2001), ABC reported that the cigarette manufacturer was promoting the consumption of cigarettes in the Czech Republic. According to ABC reports, Phillip Morris told government officials that smoking makes economic sense. Persons will die sooner smoking cigarettes so the government saves in retirement, housing, and medical costs for the elderly.

The ABC.com Web site reported that the study "was part of an ongoing debate about the economics of the cigarette excise tax policy in the Czech Republic." Philip Morris International said in a statement issued late on Monday that "Philip Morris deeply regrets any impression from this study that the premature death of smokers represents a benefit to society."

Northwest Airlines Bad Press

It was a very bad storm. On January 3, 1999 with 14 inches of snow, Northwest Airlines landed plane after plane until thirty were stranded on the tarmac at the Detroit Metropolitan Wayne County Airport. How would you like to be on a plane for up to nine hours? Plane toilets overflowed. Planes were unable to get to the gate. Passengers used their cell phones and called the CEO of Northwest in Minneapolis! One claimed he was "imprisoned." Northwest later settled with passengers for $7.15 million.

Northwest did not respond fast enough and didn't have staff levels to handle the situation.

Books

When you benchmark a non-competitor and see how they approach situations, you may pick up some ideas.

How might a publisher handle different "channels?"

❑ Use a lower grade paper for the Book of the Month Club.

❑ Let one vendor have the hard back and another have the paperback.

❑ Bundle the books for different channels. For example two of the "Dummies" books could be put together on similar topics.

What about ebooks? Many are now being published on Adobe Acrobat 5.0. How can one handle the situation where customers know that that warehouse cost for an ebook is $20 a year? Try bundling again.

Charge $27.96 for the hardback.

Charge $19.11 for the ebook. Of course, format the ebook so that it cannot be printed. Add additional value to the ebook, such as color or hyperlinks, for more information.

Charge $37.00 for them both together.

Brokerage Firms

There are 550,000 franchises in the U.S. overall. From automobile dealerships to drugstores, the market is large.

Target affinity groups

In 1977, Merrill Lynch targeted franchises starting with the 7,700 Mobil service stations.

The average Mobil dealer nets $85,000 a year. Mobil spent $250,000 to educate twenty Merrill financial consultants and to market the planning program to their franchisees. Each franchisee will have to pay $175 for a personal financial plan and $750 for a business plan. Merrill plans to offer traditional investment advice and an added service, *strategic business initiatives*, such as acquiring other stations and cutting costs. (Note: Mobil obtains 20 percent of its revenue from franchises so Mobil wants to help them succeed.)

Next Steps: This author has little doubt that Merrill will also arrange the financial packages to acquire new stations.

Best Practice

Provide a value-added business-planning service in addition to financial planning. This makes you part of the customer's enterprise, if the personal relationships are built and maintained. The key here is to maintain a trusted relationship. This cannot be done if personnel are promoted and moved to other cities.

Best Lead Generator for Financial Planners

Successful Money Management® is a nine-hour program that financial planners and brokers can license to educate the public about investing. As a result of taking the program, the prospects have more knowledge and have evaluated the presenter, who often gets business from half the class participants.

Bundling Strategy

Typically thought of as a merchandising strategy, this strategy is used more and more to capture niche markets and to influence product line strategy.

The bundling strategy is used:

❑ To move out slow moving products, for example a company must buy the entire line if they want X.

❑ To position yourself with respect to the competition in a way they cannot match. For example, a motorized manufacturer of fitness equipment bundles treadmills with stair type exercise equipment. For merchandising: Stanley Works will bundle complimentary tools.

❑ To provide unique packages to channels. For example, a Hewlett Packard printer such as their DeskWriter 600 series is about the same price at CompUSA and Office Depot. MacMall, a direct-mail catalogue for Macintosh compatible software and hardware, sold the HP DeskWriter 680C printer bundled with the CardShop Plus! DeluxCD.

❑ To provide unique value to the customer. Toro Co., to compete against (John) Deere & Co.'s attractive financing for golf course maintenance equipment, offers drip irrigation systems, turf-rollers, and lawn mowers for new golf courses. They also matched the financing.

Thomas J. DiLorenzo, a professor of economics, wrote a letter to the editor of the *Wall Street Journal* about the "Economic Joy of Bundling." He wrote:

The seller of a product knows more about that product and how it will perform with other complementary products than consumers do. Hence, bundling is also an attempt to assure that one's product performs as well a possible—an important concern in an industry as competitive as computers.

One reason why product bundling is efficient is that consumers like their products bundled and it is profitable for business to accommodate those preferences. Bundling products often sell for a lower price than if they were all sold separately, and can eliminate the costs of haggling over the prices of separate items.

Bundling can also vastly reduce the transaction costs involved in shopping around. New computers typically come equipped with dozens of software products: shopping separately for them is something few consumers care to do.

When a retailer commits to buy only from a single manufacturer it secures for both parties a planned product flow that reduces record keeping and inventory holding costs. Such contracts provide incentives for retailers to promote the product of their sole supplier, which can benefit both the manufacturer and the retailer.

Manufacturers will provide specialized training and financial assistance that helps with product promotion and service.

Exclusive dealing also increases the return to national advertising by generating more business to all dealers in the product. Exclusive dealing contracts are a way of achieving the benefits of vertical integration without investing capital in retail outlets.

Business Model

Many companies have a business model and infrastructure that does not work with current reality. Thus CompUSA, Office Depot, and Computer City watch nervously as one company after another begins to build computers to order, rather than using a retail outlet.

Some business models offer the opportunity to be used over and over again. One example is Grow Biz International.

Grow Biz International (now Winmark) sells worn, but not worn out

Located in Minnesota, Grow Biz International sells and trades recycled merchandise. They have a chain named Play It Again Sports to recycle exercise and sports equipment. Video Game Exchange and Computer Renaissance are two other chains they franchise.

In 1998 they purchased Tool Traders Inc. of Royal Oak Michigan. They plan to have five hundred stores in five years. Starting in the Detroit area they will expand through company-owned and franchise stores.

Once Upon a Child handles apparel, furniture, books, and toys. Plato's Closet deals with worn, but not worn out clothing. For example, a Rue 21 tank top that retails for $28 might be purchased used for $3 and sold for $8. In Monroeville, PA, Sue Hyde is the owner of the local Plato's Closet. She trained her employees on how to buy clothing that is in good condition. She lets her employees buy the clothes when she is not around, stating, "I give lots of empowerment to my employees (regarding what to buy) because they know what's good and in style and what's not."[18]

Amazon.com

Amazon.com started out as an on-line bookseller. Since they didn't have to charge tax and were open 24/7, they became popular. Since they carried small publishers, the on-line merchant got a lot of positive press in writing schools. They expanded into videotapes, CDs, DVDs, electronics, and now they partner with major retailers such as Target.

Capture the Aged When They Are Young

When the baby boomers were young, the top of the line car was a Cadillac. Toyota Motor Corp. came out with the low-priced Corolla. The low price pulled in first-time buyers. As time went on they came out with new models and ended up with the Lexus as the boomers got the last child through college.

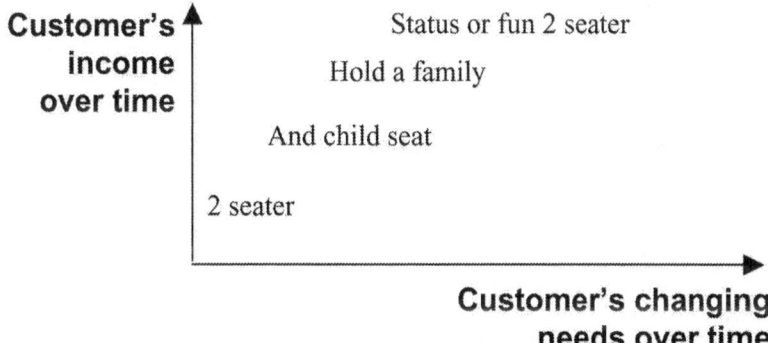

Another way to look at this is to have an offering at every price point. Vendors usually cluster around value price points. You can maintain market share and profitability by constantly providing more value at a lower price point. It eliminates the low quality/low value producers.

The absence of an offering at key price points is what enabled the Japanese and Volkswagen to capture market share in automobiles in the United States and Canon to move into the Xerox copier area.

Cartridge Entertainment

Best practice is to target eleven-to seventeen-year-old boys for use with Nintendo, Sony Playstation, and Xbox. If possible, cross-market with movies by incorporating their sound tracks into the product.

KOBI JAMES • 87

Channels of Distribution

Use All the Channels

Digi International Inc. provides connectivity products for multi-user environments (UNIX, DOS, OS/2, and Microsoft). Digi advertised in every major trade journal and PC publication to create awareness. They had a strategy of engineering excellence and building alliances with Novell, IBM, Apple, Compaq, and Microsoft.

Digi had a strong sales network of OEMs, system integrators, and value-added resellers.

Lock Up Channels

Direct sales is the most expensive channel. A common technique is to work with a major distributor and retailer, obtaining an agreement of exclusivity in exchange for privileges, thus blocking the competition.

Change Channels as the Product Matures

It is not uncommon for a product to move from something unique to a commodity. However the company does not realize this. Apple, Xerox, and P&G in their dealings with Wal-Mart all failed to see themselves as the customers saw them. A new, expensive product may need a direct sales force to communicate its unique value to the customers.

Over time, successful products, especially ones not protected by patents, will find competition. The customers will become used to the products and need less support. The products then can be sold in stores or catalogues. Eventually even telemarketing could be used when the customer perceives your product as a commodity (or at least as one of many).

Hewlett-Packard discovered this in the mid-nineties. Gas chromatographs, or GCs, were sold by a direct sales force. The sales force had over five hundred products to know. Today, chemists take classes in chromatography and often know more than the sales force. HP switched over to telesales and found the customers were still satisfied while the cost to sell the same amount of goods dropped.

Case Study: CIDCO

Cidco makes Caller IDs. Cidco's three channels include:

- ❏ Retailers such as Wal-Mart and Target to capture individual consumers,
- ❏ Telephone companies such as the baby bells, which in turn charge for a service called Caller ID, and
- ❏ The OEM market, in which they put the client's name on the product (AT&T and Radio Shack or corporate clients and individuals).

Although target customers overlap, there is differentiation by color, name, and connection. To ensure market share, CIDCO practices Kaisen—continuous improvement—and also improves their products, such as putting Caller ID on a Call Waiting Line.

Charge Cards

Why do companies want customers to use their charge cards? The data from charge cards lets us know who is buying what and thus we can have more of what they want. Customers often have a balance on their charge cards. This is very profitable. Overall sales increase when credit is made available. Last but not least, providing credit to customers leads to purchases of higher priced goods.

Kohl's

How do we encourage the use of charge cards? Kohl's has a simple technique: provide an additional 10 percent discount on all regular and sale-priced merchandise.

To encourage credit card usage there are privileges awarded. These include:

❑ Additional discounts on sales prices eight times a year. They come as invitational cards,
❑ An itemized billing statement showing exactly what you purchased, and
❑ The opportunity to obtain Kohl's "Exclusive Most Valued Customer" status.

Most Valued Customer, or MVC status, provides "EXCLUSIVE" benefits. Kohl's capitalizes the word exclusive. These EXCLUSIVE benefits include:

❑ An invitation to pick a personal sales day four times a year, and
❑ The MVC NOW Quarterly Newsletter with "useful information and valuable gifts."

Cautionary Note: If your company issues a multi-use card, such as a Visa or MasterCard, you may become liable for criminal prosecution in New York if the card is used for Internet gambling. Citibank, with over 30 million Visa and MasterCard holders, began to block the use of their cards for Internet gambling in June 2002. Fraud and delinquency rates were higher on charges used for Internet gambling. ("I didn't use the card to make the bet; someone must have stolen my PIN.")

Cobranding

Extensions

"Extensions" is a jargon word that means cross-promoting one company's network of outlets with the merchandise and goods of other companies.[19] We call that **Cobranding**. Elsewhere in the text we mentioned:

- ❏ Nestlé chocolate chip cookies at Burger King,
- ❏ Taco Bells in petrol stations and Cinnabon at Arby's,
- ❏ Mini McDonald's in Wal-Marts,
- ❏ Kiosks in stores ranging from coupon dispensers to soda can retrievers, and
- ❏ FedEx at the Post Office.

For a while Gateway had a store in Office Depot. Avon has a "store-within-a-store" at J.C. Penney. Here are some additional examples:

- ❏ TCF Banks are in Cub Foods,
- ❏ Wells Fargo & Company banks are in Safeway stores,
- ❏ FedEx is in Kinko's, and
- ❏ McDonald's experiments with Freddie Mac mortgage terminals, different branded meats, and perhaps McRetail[20] is coming to a McDonald's near you.

When Business Mentors thinks of Extensions, we think of:

- ❏ Using the old in new ways,
- ❏ Product Family extensions,
- ❏ Modifying an offering to fit into a new channel, and
- ❏ Using a Brand in a new Category. The Martha Stewart brand is excellent at this.

Martha Stewart Omnimedia has a variety of knowledge products sold in different channels.

Magazines	Media	Merchandising
Martha Stewart Living	**askMartha,** a newspaper column	**Martha Stewart Signature**, a line a specialty home products
Martha Stewart Baby	**askMartha**, a radio program	**Martha By Mail**, a catalogue
Martha Stewart Weddings	*From Martha's Kitchen*, a cable TV program	**MarthaStewart.com**, an on-line site
Books	Weekly appearance on *The Early Show* on CBS	**Martha Stewart** Everyday products for home kitchen and garden, a mass-market retail brand that can be found at K-mart, Zellers (in Canada), and Sears.
More than 30	TV specials	

Component Sharing Strategy

A favorite strategy of Briggs and Stratton engines is that they will put the engine in anything: a snow blower, a lawnmower, etc. When carried to its logical extreme you become the OEM for other manufacturers or assemblers for that component.

In 1997, IBM began to ship computers without certain parts so that the disc drive and memory could be assembled locally. The retail channel will add the last few components and be able to take advantage of drops in chip prices.

B. Joseph Pine in *Mass Customization* reports that this strategy is best used to reduce the number of parts and thus the costs associated with a product line that has a large amount of variety. He reports that Black and Decker used this approach to create *more* **variety and** *faster* **product development.**

Component Swapping Strategy

Similar to the Component Sharing Strategy, here the different components are paired with the basic product.

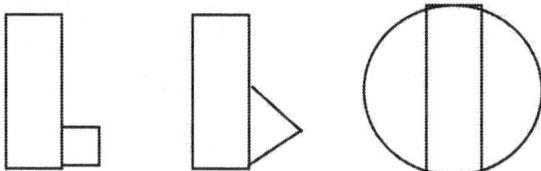

Examples include
❑ Create-A-Book® uses one story line but allows a child's name to be entered.
❑ Aircraft derivatives are the same structures but with more seats or new features or the ability to make longer non-stop flights. "So what will it be, a 737-800 or a 737-900. Or perhaps you would like to go 10,000 miles without stopping?"
❑ Swatch uses one watch and a thousand faces. An implied requirement (basic quality) is that it keeps good time. The sale is often an emotional or impulse purchase.
❑ Bowling balls are made centrally and then the fingers are drilled at your local bowling alley.
❑ Glass frames are made centrally, but the lenses are added locally.
The advantage is infinite variety and value added to the consumer of the products. The key to success is determining what should be centrally produced (the standard set of product or service) and what should be customizable.

Consolidate

In the seventies France picked a design for its nuclear power plants and then used that design over and over again. In the United States, each nuclear power plant was designed, adding to the cost.

Sometimes it is good to put all your eggs in one basket. Do this when:

❑ Large numbers of personnel need to be trained. This is why information technology groups will standardize on certain software packages. They cannot afford to support everything.

❑ You want to reduce inventory of spare parts and tools. Once upon a time all automobile headlights were circular. Then the manufacturers got permission to have square headlights. Who opposed this? Service stations trying to avoid inventory costs.

❑ You want to reduce record keeping and the number of technical manuals.

❑ Your total cost of ownership, the purchase price and maintenance expenses, decreases. According to a Boeing Press Release in 2002, their 737 maintenance costs are up to 35 percent lower than the A320 series as reported by the U.S. Department of Transportation Form 41, an FAA-required form on which airlines report their costs.

❑ You have a "fleet" of planes, trucks, or cars and you wish to simplify fleet management. When problems occur, you can easily substitute one (car, plane, engine, server) for another.

Core Competencies

The greatest area of weakness in business is in Project Management. This is a core competency needed for launching new products, building new facilities, implementing new application software, etc. This should be required training. Successful companies focus on this and on interpersonal relationships.

Creative Innovation

Creative innovation is seeing what is going on in one industry and recognizing that you could do it in your industry.

Henry Ford reportedly saw the way beef is slaughtered with one man after another working on a line and created the assembly line.

The founder of Staples, an office supply store, saw the advantages of bar coding and supermarket variety and applied those in a radical way to a different business.

Creative Innovation provides opportunity to the company that goes first if you are a learning organization that can profit from mistakes and misadventure. **It often provides value to the customer in:**

- ❑ **Reduced cost** as when electronic data interchange was first offered.
- ❑ **Ease of use**, as when Eastern Airlines launched its Sabre System of making reservations. Travel agents rushed to sign up because prior to a centralized reservation system that showed many flights, the old method was to call each airline.
- ❑ **Special value**, as when PCH provided pharmacies with printouts of typical drug interactions. Now a pharmacy could provide drug interaction information to customers.

Note that the above three were very important leaps forward, but today are commonplace.

If you cannot have Creative Innovation, have Creative Imitation.

- ❑ Federated Department Stores, the parent company of Macy's and Bloomingdale's, opened its department store of the future, Bon Marche. (One reporter said it looked like a Kohl's!)
- ❑ A vendor of "we come to you" car washes was losing money because clients were canceling appointments. He copied the practice of his karate coach. The coach made the students pay on the first day of the month. The car washer made his customers pay on the first and he no longer has customers skipping appointments.

Customer Partnership

Toro

In addition to attractive financing, Toro provides services such as accounting, insurance, marketing support, and employee training to lawn maintenance contractors. [21]

Xerox

Xerox wasn't sure about how a document publishing system would be used, so it made certain customers partners and developed applications.

OEM for Others

Training companies, equipment manufacturers, bakeries, etc. will put your label, your logo, a special icing on the product to make it look like it is yours to your customers. Mass customization is the key to high profits. The greater the degree of commonality, the higher the profits will be. When you become the OEM for others you should gain economies of scale that make it harder for your competition to compete on price.

Customer Profits

Pareto

It is common knowledge that 80 percent of your profits come from 20 percent of your customers. Or is it? Are you measuring it? Perhaps 80 percent of your revenue is coming from 20 percent of your customers. Because of discounting, your largest customers may be costing you money!

One analysis showed that 80 percent of the profit did come from 22 percent of the customers. However, 30 percent of the profit came from the next 65 percent of the customers. Accountants will note that this adds up to 110 percent profit. The remaining 15 percent of the customers were costing 10 percent of the profits. When hearing this story, one distributor of energy quickly realized that even though revenues were up and the number of customers was up, profits were down. "Damn," he shouted aloud in one of our workshops. "My competitor is sending me his high cost customers." He was right.

Richard Harmer, a senior fellow at Framingham, Massachusetts consultants Strategic Pricing Group said, "Nine out of ten of our clients find they aren't making any profit on the customers they thought were their bread and butter."

Get the Family Money Together

Autonomy was the key in business. Let each division plant have autonomy. Today, the key is the larger the purchase, the larger the discount. Thus HMOs can get larger discounts than an individual hospital. Divisions can combine purchasing and get better prices.

Customer Satisfaction

Customer satisfaction is often not what is measured. The quality movement has produced consistency across industries. When you always get what you expect, satisfaction becomes something other than the product.

At Burger King, customer satisfaction drops if the food does not arrive within three minutes. After four minutes, the level of satisfaction drops off and it "goes way down at five."[22]

Your vendors (channels) are customers, too. McDonald's franchisers grumbled that the Arch Deluxe sandwich took too long to assemble for the profit it generated.

By capturing the spoken or expressed voice of the customer, you can identify what will truly impact customer satisfaction.

Best Practice

Any survey must ask about *overall satisfaction*.

Key Reading

Harvard Business Review based upon Xerox Corp. research, 1995, "Why Satisfied Customers Defect" by Thomas Jones and W. Earl Sasser Jr.

Defeaturing

Defeaturing an offering can capture a price sensitive segment of the marketplace by replacing nice-to-have features with must-have features. It can extend the life of technology that is rapidly changing. Similar to remanufacturing, clients expect a price break.

Defeatured Notebook Saves Hundreds		
Defeaturing is useful to target specific markets. For example, sales persons, trainers, and shop floor supervisors do not need DVD players and do not need the power that engineering staff may require.	1.0 GHz AMD	1.4 GHz Pentium 4
	128MB ram	256 MB ram
	20 GB HD	20 GB HD
	CD-R	DVD/CD-RW
	56 K Modem	56 K Modem
	10/100 Ethernet	10/100 Ethernet
	$789	$1449

Realistic Street Prices July 2002 including all rebates

The expensive notebook above has a faster processing speed and a DVD player. Except the client has no need for a DVD player. Vendors say, "Soon the software will be coming out on DVDs. You may need it." They have been saying that since 2001.

The Everything Old Is New Again Strategy

Nostalgia can be sold. The recapturing of old, good feelings creates hits.

❑ The Chrysler Cruiser has a retro look.

❑ Mattel brought back its Rock'em Sock'em Robots in the spring of 2001. Using the concept of Product Family Planning there was also a set of action figures, and a video game for Sony's PlayStation 2.

❑ The Saturn Sport Coupe of the early nineties with its flip-up headlights was really a poor man's Corvette.

❑ Every year at Hess Gas Stations they release a toy truck with their logo. The nostalgic father buys one for his son.

Extend the Selling Cycle   Profit Strategies

Nordstrom's has their only sale, their really big sale, on August 1. You can buy your winter clothes while it is still summer and have the fashion you want on the first day of fall.

Hallmark Crown Stores begin to sell their Christmas figurines July 15.

What do these two practices have in common? This enables the two retailers to see what is hot, providing them the opportunity to order more from overseas manufacturers. Even including the six-week shipping time from the Far East, they will have ample time to receive additional shipments.

Extend Offering into New Channels   Profit Strategies

Oreo® cookies can be purchased in grocery stores in their two-row, soft-sided containers, in single-row cardboard boxes in most hotel gift shops, and now as single wrapped cookies served with an airline "meal." This is the strategy of being scalable, or resizing the offering for different channels. Other Scalable or "Cut to Length" strategies include salad bars and fabric stores.

Nestlé's Toll House cookie dough came in a tube, then in precut squares. In 2002, they took the dough and made it bigger to sell Toll House Chocolate Chip Cookies in Burger King Restaurants.

False Front (Faux Front)

With the false front, the inside is the same but the cover is different. The goal is to target something of interest to your customer that your offering would support.

Next time you are in the supermarket, look at magazine rack of *TV Guide*s. Chances are there will be different covers on the same issue!

Stockbrokers can do the same with mutual funds. The brochures have different covers, one for retirees and one for college funds.

Holiday cards do it. There is one common greeting with your name printed at the bottom.

Several catalogue printers put information that would be of interest to the customer (on the address label) on the first five to fifteen pages, and then the rest of the catalogue is the same for everyone.

- ❑ Horticulture—place annuals or products suitable for the customer's growing zone up front.
- ❑ Agriculture—place better seeds up front based upon last year's purchases.
- ❑ Clothing—What has this customer purchased before? Put similar styles up front.

Getting Close to Customers

Customer Appreciation

In West Bloomington, MN on December 3, 1998 they had a Customer Appreciation Day. Good cookies, fresh coffee, and a smiling letter carrier greeted people as they came into the post office lobby. Yes, the Post Office!

Saturn

At the Saturn dealership they are serving hot dogs and giving a free seminar on how the car works.

Partner With the Customer or Your Vendor

There are many ways to get close to your customers. Some companies partner with their clients. This can be used to reduce the cost of bringing something to market. It can be used to make an offering better before it is released. Xerox partnered with key customers to identify a better way to use their DocuPrint printers.

A pharmaceutical company is working with Learning International to create a course. Learning International can resell it to non-pharmaceutical companies.

New York Life partnered with Wilson Learning to use Wilson's customer-centered sales curriculum for their agents. The agents' sales doubled! Even in downturns of the marketplace, the trained agents' revenue was twice that of their untrained counterparts.

Software companies release beta versions over the Internet for thousands of customers to beta test. Feedback identifies usages and problems not anticipated by the programmers.

Goals

To reach a goal, you must have staff skilled in the work to be performed and a documented plan to accomplish the goal. The goal must be measurable, with clear milestones to indicate that progress is occurring as planned.

Goal Setting Guidelines:

- ❑ Goals should have a measurable outcome. You begin with the end in mind. If it is not measurable, you will not be able to agree with others that the goal has been obtained.
- ❑ There should be a clear set of steps with people assigned to each step.
- ❑ The people assigned to the steps must have the skill set to perform the work. (Availability is not a skill set.)
- ❑ There must be milestones along the way that indicate progress towards the goal.
- ❑ There should be a celebration when the goal has been met.

Project Management is a skill set for accomplishing goals.

Often we find that financial plans (numbers) are not based in reality. For example, a company needs a specific profit margin. Failure to meet the profit margin will mean the stock price will not increase and a large number of projects will be cancelled. To ensure the profit margins are met, sales reduces its SAG expenses, at least on paper. However, when asked how the SAG expenses is going to move from 27 percent of sales down to 22 percent of sales, the response is "we will make it happen." There is no plan on how to do it. At the end of next year, the profit margin had not been met.

Playing with numbers on a spreadsheet is not goal setting. The use of spreadsheets and "what if" analyses is meant only to help you understand the impact of certain strategies.

Grocery stores

Entry to Store

Entryways are considered decompression zones. At a Giant superstore in Camp Hill, Pa, the first thing a shopper sees is cactus plants, an impulse buy with a high profit margin. At Wegmans in Webster, NY, the shoppers view rows of brightly colored plants and fruits on low tables, with a pizza bar on the left and homemade breads on the right. The vision is an oasis of food and the odors awaken the taste buds and start the gastric juices flowing so that the customers buy more. All of the fruits are at waist height, making selection easy.

Best designs make the shoppers turn to the right and wander through a maze. With the average store time of twenty-two minutes, the goal is to get the customer to make impulse purchases. It is standard to put milk at the rear of the store to increase traffic.

Collocate Fixings

A common practice is to place the pasta and olive oil near the vegetables so that all the ingredients are close together. The Giant Eagle supermarket chain keeps five of eight dozen egg cartons next to the bacon.

Food courts

Many supermarkets include eating areas that are the quality of Denny's or Perkins. Customers can eat in or take home a prepared meal. Byerly's, in St. Louis Park, MN, has an eat-in restaurant and takeout Chinese food made buy a local restaurant. Wegmans, in Webster, NY, also has the takeout Chinese food, but it is their own brand. These prepared meals are a direct response to the Boston Market type franchises.

Whine Factor

Cookies are at kid height so that parents, guilty of not spending enough quality time with their kids, purchase if the kids complain. Also, 22 percent of shoppers are dads. To get parents to go down cookie aisles, place baby food or juices on the opposite side.

Store brands

The eyes move from left to right, so put the store brand on the right of, or between, two national brands.

Checkout Lines

At rush hour, push high-profit items like magazines, bottles of cold soda, and candy at the third person back in the line, where customers have a chance to browse. The second person in line is impatiently waiting and rarely browses.

Candy-Free Lines

To be parent friendly, many stores will have candy-free checkout lanes.

Endcaps

Good endcaps in the front or rear can increase sales. In the front they can pull customers across the store. In the rear, people often brush up against them, leading to impulse buys. In one study, coffee sales increased 567 percent when put at an endcap. (Source: Point of Purchase Institute)

Parent Friendly

The trend for 2003 will be for stores to offer a children's play area that is supervised. The parent and child receive matching wrist bracelets and the parent can leave the child for up to ninety minutes. This approach has been used in health clubs since 1995.

Hotels

The key to success in the lodging business is to watch Marriott. They are the best at benchmarking and identifying differences in price points and amenities.

Basic Quality

Using the Kano model, the basic requirements for business travelers, regardless of price point include:

- ❑ Safety,
- ❑ Cleanliness,
- ❑ Accuracy of bill and reservation,
- ❑ Television, and
- ❑ Wake-up (call or alarm clock)

Best Practices

Move into a related field: Hotels can also run family resorts, tours, and vacation getaways. The Stakis Group of Scotland, for example, operates casinos and golf resorts.

Develop a brand name or names that define a level of service and quality.

Keep a local flavor. HFS has the brands of Ramada, Days Inn, and Howard Johnson. Does anyone want to go to Madrid and stay in a Days Inn? Even business travelers appreciate local charm. Give the amenities of a Days Inn price point, but keep the Spanish entrees. For European chains coming to North America, bring some of your charm and you will win big.

Innovation

Great Harvest

At Great Harvest Bread Co. the cover page of the franchise contract states in bold letters:

ANYTHING
not expressly prohibited by
the language in this agreement
IS ALLOWED.

While a franchise must make bread out of whole wheat and sell it hot to the customers, there are no restraints on what can be done. As a result the business owners communicate with each other and innovations run through the system. Or perhaps we should say e-mail through the system. The **stores that seem to innovate the best regularly "talk"** to three or five other stores and have another network of ten stores. What works gets passed on.

In Style Magazine

She was frustrated when she looked in fashion magazines but could not find out how to obtain the fashions she saw. David Carr wrote in the *New York Times* that that the founding editor of *In Style* magazine took "fashion out of the runways of Paris and onto the runway of life." Martha Nelson, the founding editor of *In Style*, created a niche when she combined two topics that had been separate: fashion and celebrity. She not only displayed the fashion but also explained where and how to get it, using a celebrity to model the new clothes or the hairstyle.

Kano Examples of the Wow-Sizzle Feature or Attribute

Having the ability to get ice or water in the refrigerator door is a sizzle feature, as any parent will attest. It isn't a patent, it is a technology and it is in the higher-priced refrigerators.

Kodak had a sizzling product in the fall of 2001. Their digital cameras called Easy Share were just that, easy to share. Kodak made it easy to get the digital photos from the camera to the PC. They took a customer difficulty—downloading photos—and made it easy.[23]

Intuit's Quicken Money is always innovating. It holds a 70 to 78 percent market share in the United States even though it competes with Microsoft Money.

Lawn Care

Target Buyers

Target mailings to desirable demographic and geographic groups that can afford the service. (This is a best practice for any mailing!) This will guarantee a higher response rate than a general mailing would produce.

Sell Additional Services

Sell additional services such as tree and shrub care. **Barefoot**, the #2 professional lawn care provider in the United States, diversified into commercial plant care in 1995.

Learning Organization

At AOL the Customer Service Center in Jacksonville, Florida isn't staffed with computer science majors; it is staffed with caring people. (Not that a computer science geek couldn't also be a caring person.) They have a database with hundreds of solutions to customers' problems at their fingertips. In addition to helping the customers, they help the AOL engineers. They track the customers' problems so that the engineers know what is causing pain. Every week, senior executives get a report on customer satisfaction, the types of calls, and how they were resolved.

"Where is the file I downloaded?" or "How to I send a picture to grandma?"

When AOL software version six was released, 40 percent of the changes were "Promoted by customer feedback."[24]

Project Management is a tool to share "how we have done things" with other employees and functional areas.

"Lego ®" or Sectional Modularity Strategy

The Lego ® Strategy is named after Lego building blocks. In this strategy you have a series of components and assemble them to make different products or services.

Japanese Software

The book *Japanese Software Factories* describes how the Japanese were using factory-like approaches to software. They would **write modules and use them over and over again in different applications.** The result was error-free software because the bugs had been discovered on earlier projects.

Wendy's

Do want a hamburger or a double hamburger,

without cheese
or with cheese?

Logical Extensions

You can outgrow your competition by looking at what your logical growth would be. The strategy is to look at your core competencies and use them in new and creative ways. It is evolutionary.

In the seventies, companies bought up companies to smooth the revenue flow. Thus if you were in a cyclical business you would buy something that could help your business cash flow. So a copier company bought an insurance company; and a chemical giant got into financial services. The trouble was that these companies did not know how to run the other businesses.

Mindmapping is a tool that can help you see where you could be. As an example, let's look at Marriott. What are some of their competencies?

- ❑ Managing hotel properties
- ❑ Managing food services
- ❑ Managing banquets (e.g. business conventions, weddings, school reunions)
- ❑ Managing reservations
- ❑ Developing hotel segments (e.g. Marriott Courtyard)
- ❑ Training and development of entry-level personnel

Marriott

An example of a Mindmap for Marriott based upon competencies:

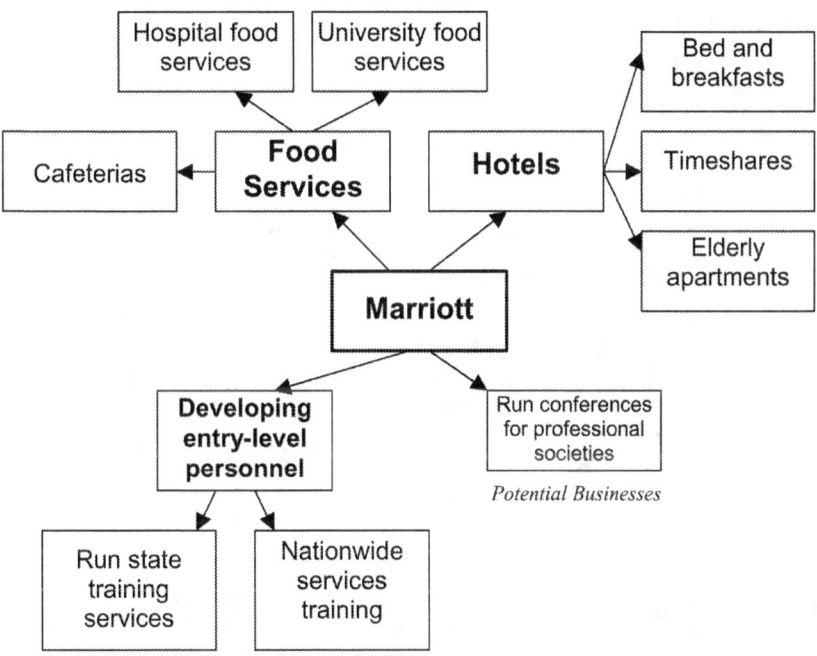

Potential Businesses

Another approach to using core competencies is to look at asset utilization. That's how UPS got into the air-passenger business. Last but not least is to **track what your customers are requesting and provide it.**

Oakwood Homes

Oakwood Homes Corp. was founded in 1946. There was an IPO in 1971. The company grew until the oil crisis hit Texas, where Oakwood had expanded. Massive home foreclosures that occurred in 1987–8 hurt the company. It has since diversified into eighteen states.

So what type of businesses would a single section homebuilder be in? The graphic below shows the actual corporation.

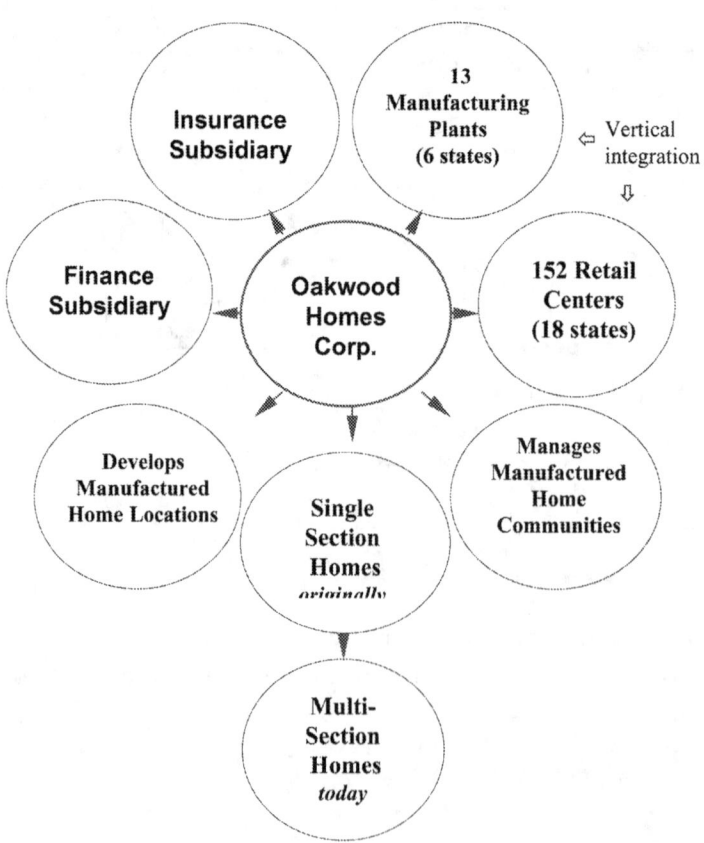

Manufacturing

Best Practice

Design in one location but build in three. Multinationals should have plants worldwide when:

- ❑ Natural or civil disturbances need to be minimized.
- ❑ Local content or balance of trade issues need to be addressed.
- ❑ Spoilage is an issue.

The Critical Six

Manufacturing engineers need to know:

- ❑ Statistical Process Control
- ❑ Kaban (JIT)
- ❑ Cycle time reduction—Lean Manufacturing
- ❑ Design for standardization
- ❑ Design for assembly
- ❑ Value analysis tool set including fail-safeing.

The reduction in inventory, faster WIP, and reduced waste adds to the bottom line for companies that use these practices.

Managed Care

(Health care in homes, supplies to homes, nursing homes)
Common practice for the remainder of the this decade will be to go into small communities to avoid competition. Getting deep discounts from care providers can cover small business. By having financial models to assist in pricing and service delivery, you will appeal to larger managed care providers who may not enter the market.

Manage the Business

Firms are sprouting up to manage the business end of specialty clinics and independent practice associations (IPAs). The key here is to relieve physicians from the administrative side of the business.

Marketing

The Offering is #1. Marketing is a tool. Marketing is about relationships. "Be at the right place, at the right time, in front of the right customers."

Marketing has been called the truth made interesting, communicated to those who would be interested.

Marketing best practice—Affinity Groups

Marketing to affinity groups is becoming more of an art form. New York City based N2K's Music Boulevard sells music, video, and other merchandise on the Web at www.musicblvd.com. It allows 11,000 small music Web sites to link to musicblvd.com. So if you want to set up a Web site on the music group 'N Sync (popular with teenage girls), you can list their CDs and when somebody orders the CD they get taken to musicblvd.com. When someone goes to musicblvd.com and purchases a product, 7 to 15 percent of the revenue goes back to the referring site.

A Web site devoted to affinity programs exists at refer-it.com. Thus a small manufacturer can be promoted by being referred by others.

Marketing Analysis Tool—Mix Modeling

Mix Modeling has evolved from techniques developed by packaged goods marketers over the past decade to become the most reliable and widely accepted means of measuring the efficiency of marketing elements.

Using statistical techniques known as econometrics, Mix Modeling is capable of determining the contribution of each individual element to driving product sales or other outcomes. Such techniques can "decompose" or attribute the sales derived from specific advertising media, direct mail drops, promotional programs, or personal sales efforts over a given time period. Mix Modeling can decompose outcomes as short term as monthly sales volume or as long term as multi-year brand equity growth or decay.

Westhill Marketing Sciences has developed the MarCom Simulator™. With this tool product mix plans can be tested, budgets optimized, and business forecasted. (Westhill Marketing Sciences, 85 Fifth Avenue, New York, NY 10003, Phone: 212-243-2100)

Medical: Hospitals

Hospitists

In order to keep physicians in their offices seeing patients, many hospitals have MDs that take care of the patients while they are in the hospital. They are on salary and work with the primary care physician.

Mergers and Acquisitions

The secret here is to only acquire value-added companies, technologies, market access, or distribution channels. As a consultant I ask, what is the exact bottom-line figure you expect to get (not hope to get or wish to get)? "Expect to get" is what an average MBA student would agree to if you showed her the figures.

Microsoft

Of course, there will be exceptions. For example, Microsoft will buy a small company, not for the application or computer code, but for the people. When the programmers are also the stockholders, Microsoft has essentially paid a sign-on bonus and captured the talent. A key learning point here is that people always are important. Whether buying a technology or a channel, the people make the difference.

CVS

On the other hand, CVS, a drug store chain located in upscale neighborhoods, will buy a competitor's prescription list, but not the pharmacy or the store. CVS has a business model that if the customer comes in for medication, they will buy another $30-$50 worth of products.

HFS Inc.

Sometimes an acquisition can make synergy exist where none existed before. HFS Inc. was one such example. HFS has residential and real estate operations. It franchised about 12,000 Caldwell Banker, Century 21, and ERA real estate offices. However, it does not issue mortgages. In 1995, HFS sold properties worth $80 billion in mortgages. HFS also owns Avis Rent-A-Car and Days Inn hotel franchises. How can HFS get synergy from its companies? It purchased PHH, a corporate relocation service that is also involved in long-term auto leasing. In essence, it has vertical integration. PHH will direct customers to HFS's Century 21, Days Inn, and Avis units. Time will tell if this 1996 strategy is well implemented.

Movie Theatres

Use assets in new ways:

- ❑ Rent space for meetings.
- ❑ Use the back of the ticket for advertisements—General Cinema charged Tommy Hilfiger $85,000 to promote its Freedom cologne on 3 million tickets.
- ❑ Don't run commercials for other companies. Show more previews.
- ❑ Connect with customers in new ways, such as through selling tickets on-line so that they can skip the line.

Niche: Have One

Technology Niche

Avid Technology allows you to capture, edit, and distribute digital media. Users include TV studios, sports teams, and animation or entertainment companies.

Quality Systems Inc. and its NextGen Healthcare Information Systems subsidiary develop and market health care information systems that automate medical and dental group practices.

Their creativity includes writing software for PDAs that doctors can use.

PDA stands for Personal Digital Assistant, but soon they might be called Physician's Digital Assistant if Quality Systems Inc. continues to be so successful.)

Image © 2001 Quality Systems Inc. www.qsii.com

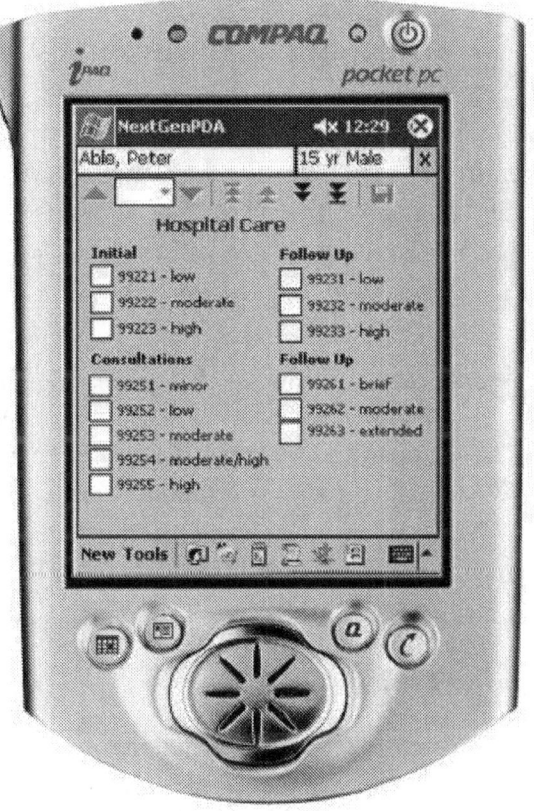

Outsource niche

Benchmark Electronics, Inc. assembles printed circuit boards, specializing in surface-mounted technology.

Benchmark is an outsource favorite for short runs.

Entertainment

BET Holdings focuses on black entertainment. Starting as a cable channel, it has expanded into movies, publishing, radio, and a jazz cable channel (1994).

Home Parties

Everyone has heard of Tupperware parties. A 1990 University of Chicago study showed that 97 percent of party attendees buy something. That is attributed to the social pressure.[25] The sales reps get a sliding scale commission of up to 30 percent. So how creative have people been in this channel?

- ❑ Pampered Chef Ltd., an Addison, Ill. kitchenware supplier, claims 30,000 U.S. consultants. Started in 1980, sales were $328 million in 1996.
- ❑ Herbs and vitamins are sold in house parties. Candles, computers, and lingerie are, too.
- ❑ Antioch Co.'s Creative Memories group had sales of $110 million selling photographic scrapbooks (1997). Founded in St. Cloud, Minn. in 1987, the company had over 24,000 representatives.

What would be your idea of a great Home Party product? I know what you are thinking—it does not make sense for your offering. If car manufacturers like Saturn can throw a barbecue for car buyers, show them how to take care of their car, and invite them to tours of the plant, perhaps the idea of a modified Home Party does make sense!

Product Niche

You can have a niche and be ignored by your competition. New Balance, don't call them tennis shoes, offers shoes in **different widths**. There is no special patent here, just a better fit for Baby Boomers' feet.

Open Platform Modularity

Open platform is a philosophical approach that says "This needs to be as flexible as possible. How do we do it?" How do we play all tapes (VHS, PAL, Secam)? How do we have one platform for all our cars? Or how do we get more business for our twenty-five injection molding machines?

Open Platform Modularity gives the vendor maximum leverage in markets and permits customization.

- ❑ Java, a programming language from Sun Microsystems, permits applications to be written once and then run on any system.
- ❑ Linux, an operating system, is basically free. Microsoft Office does not run on it, however, the free Star Office does.
- ❑ ISO, ASTM, IEEE, ANSI standards permit goods and services to be trusted.

Patents

Sony

It is estimated that Sony Corp. gets 10 percent of its revenue from licensing patents.

License

License arrangements can create Awareness and provide you with revenue that far exceeds the work involved.

Permission Marketing

IMT Strategies reports "77 percent of people delete unsought e-mail without reading it." But through Permission Marketing, asking if potential customers would be willing to receive information, e-mail can be used for low-cost and effective advertising.

Example of an e-mail sent by Loehmann's to a person who opted in to receive e-mail notices.

Lowe's has a variety of opt-in e-mail newsletters.

Piggyback

To Piggyback is to put something on something else's back. This strategy is seen manifested in alliances and sometimes in technology. There is always value added to both parties involved and to the customer. In bundling there may not be real advantage to the customer, as when the customer must take some of Product X to get Product Y.

Motorola

The benchmark technology example was the Motorola pager group. There was a subsidiary called EMBARC Communication Services, which developed and sublicensed branded information services to paging companies who transmitted the information services with traditional numeric and alphanumeric paging services. Motorola used this strategy to link with ESPN and send sport scores to pagers, calling the service ESPNet.

Planned Communities

The keys to success include identifying the characteristics of your target audience. Thus a mobile home park in Arizona or Florida does not match the needs of a fifty-five plus baby boomer who wants to have the grandkids over.

Always consider:

- ❑ Safety
- ❑ Ease of transportation for domestic help
- ❑ Cleanliness
- ❑ Availability of common areas
- ❑ Neighborliness
- ❑ Access to recreation

Benchmark

Disney's Celebration, FL is "a bit like walking onto a movie set" reported *USA Today* because "everything is perfect."[26]

Children can go downtown by themselves and people wave to one another.

You don't have to paint the white picket fences; they are a man-made material.

People come to Celebration because they want to build a community and a good life for their children.

Positioning

As Central Europe established itself with a strong middle class, its purchasing power was not lost upon European retailers and manufacturers. How businesses were positioning themselves is interesting and worthy of notice for niche marketing as cultural norms change.

What is an example of a cultural norm change? Examples of when cultural norms changed include: Germany with the fall of the Berlin Wall; the United States on September 11, 2001, the date of the terrorists attack on the World Trade Towers; in Europe December 2001 through 2002 with the introduction of the Euro.

Imagine being able to see family members that had been separated by a wall. Imagine being occupied and then being free. Joy. Excitement. Tears. Germany was now whole after having been divided since WWII.

In the United States the attack on the World Trade Towers changed everything. Rage. Fear. Revenge. Justice. The world did not expect America's response.

Imagine being seventy-eight years old and having to learn a new currency. Everything changed with the introduction of the Euro as a currency. Confusion. Fear. Anger. It used to be that automobiles were less expensive in Spain because per capita income was lower there. Now, with everything expressed in Euros, perhaps you might want to vacation in Spain and drive back in a new car.

Cultural norms change the person's world. Major waves of change usually continue for two years, with ripples lasting up to ten years. The original event can be as subtle as the moment Rosa Parks, a black woman, refused to give up her seat on a bus; it can be as radical as when the Western European government leaders joined together and said it was time to stop ethnic genocide in Eastern Europe.

What follows are three examples of how companies repositioned themselves in Eastern Europe after the fall of the Iron Curtain. This information came from *Business Week*, an excellent source for competitive information, and then the companies Web sites.

Home (Can't build a house? Why not redo your apartment?)

- ❑ Ikea Holdings—The Swedish manufacturer of home furnishings encouraged renovating your socialist-era apartment in Poland.

❑ Potten and Pannen—The Czech marketer of high-end cookware promoted sparkling new kitchens.

Financial Services (We need to save for our future.)

❑ There was still a concern about using banks; however, the push for using plastic and keeping savings in banks was strongly encouraged. "Don't carry cash, it can be stolen—use debit or credit cards instead." In order to reform Poland's state pension system, six million people had to go with a private fund.

Leisure (Let's travel and have some fun.)

❑ Malev, Bonton Lot, Lufthansa—You used to be stuck behind the Iron Curtain. Now that the borders are open it is time to see the world!

Pricing

Raise Prices

Some companies use price increases to spur wholesale buying and lift sales in the near term. Wholesalers often will purchase large quantities of product. They will then raise their prices as the manufacturer does, making additional money on the spread. Freddy's, a personal products retailer in Rochester, New York in the eighties, would only purchase products when on sale from the manufacturer.

The risk is "stuffing the channel" and having decreased sales later in the year.

Some industries plan annual increases. Wholesalers and retailers will advertise to "purchase now to get last year's prices." And they mean it.

Do you have a credit card at a special 5.2 percent interest rate? Many credit card companies raise the interest rate if you only make the minimum payment, or are even a day late.

Private Label

While manufacturers like 3M and Sony have patents, retail chains have private label goods. Think of a private label as a combination of a patent with a brand. The Gap pioneered it. The goal with a private label is to have an offering that will *live* in the store for a long time. Since customers cannot purchase it anywhere else, they are tied to the store. For example Williams-Sonoma **is** creating private label **transferware**. These pie plates, turkey platters, and gourmet kitchen products take kitchen creations into the dining room.

Why Have a Private Label?

Private labels usually have a lower SAG (Sales, Administration, and General) expense ratio than branded goods. If one knows the manufacturer of the private label, sales can actually increase. For example, the Sears sales representative will quickly point out which Kenmore washers are manufactured by Whirlpool, implying Whirlpool quality at a reduced price. To the consumer, a private label is often at a lower price, yet has a comparable quality.

The grocery store chain Shop and Save sells HomeBest "Century" high potency vitamins at $9 per 300 capsules. The advertised Centrum was $9 for 130. What is the difference? The pharmacist said the only difference was the price. "Why so much cheaper?" we asked. "No advertising, no sales person, no promotions, no lunches with the salesperson," the pharmacist replied.

Cosmetics Are Often Private Labeled

Wal-Mart Stores launched a private-label cosmetics line called No Boundaries in March 2001. It is targeted at teens, a "capture the elderly when they are young" strategy.

Target Corp. introduced a cosmetic line called Sonia Kashuk Professional Makeup in 1999.

Avon, for its store-within-a-store at J.C. Penney launched *beComing* in 2001.

Wal-Mart pursues a strategy of identifying overpriced consumer goods to create a private label. It will even buy a manufacturer. For example, Wal-Mart purchased White Cloud.

Now its two-ply toilet paper is priced much less than the competition. They introduced White Cloud diapers as an alternative to the more expensive Huggies brand.

Other examples of private brands include:

❑ Soda, detergent—Sam's Choice
❑ Girls clothing—Mary Kate and Ashley apparel (a branded private label)

Note: Mary Kate and Ashley clothing is part of a "capturing the elderly while they are young" strategy. J.C. Penney tries to capture teenage girls with its private label Arizona Jeans. Girls are important because as women they set purchase patterns.

This is even truer for Hispanic cultures in the U.S. Women do the shopping. In 2001 a "Get Milk" commercial was called daring for showing a Hispanic father *shopping* with his daughter. There was no mother shown! Fathers do not shop! Needless to say Hispanic fathers stayed glued to the commercial. (The commercial made it clear that the milk was for mother who was at home making a three-milk cake.)

Exclusivity

If not a private brand, retailers are demanding to be a sole channel for a specific product. Thus if Mattel Inc. sells to Wal-Mart some of its top-selling toys for the fall toy season, what are the 1,400 mall-based KB Toys and Toys "R" Us stores to do?

⭐ TOYS'R'US EXCLUSIVE [1] Toys "R" Us demands an exclusive product. After all, Toys "R" Us carries the entire Mattel line of toys for the other nine months of the year

If you wanted the $20 Lefty the Donkey by Ty in December 2001, you had to go to _____ (where)?

Remember to contractually specify how exclusive offerings are to be advertised.

---

[1] © 2001 Toys R Us

Public Utilities

The Yankee Group, a Boston research firm, says that 25 percent of the utilities plan to broaden into energy and telecommunications. What does this mean?

- ❑ In Detroit Lakes, Minnesota, the city's electric utility is installing fiber optics. It is better than copper at simultaneously carrying both data and electricity. They got tired of waiting for the telecommunication companies to get into the act. In Detroit Lakes, the utility can offer long-distance service, but not dial tone. The state legislature will decide just how much and how fast rural Minnesota will be wired into the twenty-first century. The local utilities are ready now to offer cable TV, phone, Internet access, and of course, electricity. They maintain that the benefits to the consumer are lower rates, local control, and the money stays local.
- ❑ Marshall, Minnesota joined Schwan's Sales Enterprises Inc., one of the city's largest employers, in jointly building a fiber network that was completed in 1994.
- ❑ In Pueblo, Colorado, the local electrical company offers AT&T service, Internet, and ADT Home Security.
- ❑ In Firestone, Colorado, the gas company, KN Energy Service, has two dozen retail services and offers wireless internet, MCI long distance, and Echostar satellite TV.[27]

The actions are prompting private businesses to serve the smaller markets with the latest technology. They are also prompting the telecommunications industry to lobby state governments to prohibit local government from serving their constituents (make that stealing customers). Missouri prohibits municipally owned utilities from getting into telecommunications.

Other ventures include:

- ❑ NSP (Northern States Power) offers appliance warranties and repair.
- ❑ Smart meters let consumers know when they are using high-priced power.
- ❑ Utilities installing central cooling and wind power.
- ❑ Telephone service is being offered over the power lines.

To reduce costs energy utility companies are:

- ❑ Installing cost-saving meters that radio usage to a retransmitter, eliminating the meter reader function.
- ❑ Selling energy efficient light bulbs or rebates on light bulbs is sponsored by utility companies to reduce the need for new power plants.
- ❑ Providing smart meters to let consumers know when they are using high-priced power

Reframing

Reframing is repositioning. It changes the concept by changing how people perceive the item.

Filter cigarettes were for women until the Marlboro Man (a cowboy) rode in from the west.

A beef processor said, "We don't say the meat was irradiated. We call it cold pasteurization."

Rental Property

There are a number of creative ways to raise the rent and make money. Higher rents have always been charged for better views (woods, pool) and higher views. The nineties have introduced some new wrinkles.

- ❑ Monitor water usage and charge accordingly.
- ❑ Install an exercise room.
- ❑ Place washers and dryers in the apartment.
- ❑ Beautify the complex with plants and flowers.
- ❑ Keep public areas clean (not just one cleaning a day).

Creative ways to make money include:

- ❑ Issuing Visa cards.
- ❑ Providing phone services.
- ❑ Offering Cable TV; Pay-TV
- ❑ Offering TV security.
- ❑ Write leases for odd durations
- ❑ Have several furnished apartments for lease or rent to resident's guests.
- ❑ Providing cleaning services.

Retail

There are three major elements for retail success.

The Right Concept: The retailer needs to have merchandise that reflects the store image so that its targeted customers have a reason to visit. For Example, K-Mart needs to have women's slacks with an elastic waist; Talbot's needs to have professional women's clothes. You will be told you have the right concept by having repeat customers.

Execution: There need to be processes in place that range from distribution and supply chain management to loyalty programs. It is critical to have sufficient inventory to meet demand, yet not have too much and excessive carrying costs. The latter can result in markdowns. Processes need to be staffed by critical people—people with the clout to make sure the processes are implemented and kept up-to-date. Execution is like a two-wheel bicycle. One wheel is the Process; the other wheel is the Process Owner. If either wheel is flat or missing, execution fails.

Management: There needs to be a keen awareness of merchandising and implementing programs that improve profitability and revenue. Management needs to understand what drives revenue. Too often in companies, ranging from Lucent to Xerox, the CEO did not understand the business.[2] Some programs can be subtle, yet impact the branding of the retailer. Bed Bath and Beyond, Kohl's, and Target are noted for store cleanliness.

---

[2] Bossidy, Larry and Charan, Ram. "Execution: The Discipline of Getting Things Done." *Crown Business.* 2002

Retail Loyalty

Personal Shoppers

Personal shoppers provide services to customers that include:
- ❑ Purchasing gifts for the client,
- ❑ Maintaining measurements of the client,
- ❑ Reminding the client of important anniversaries, and
- ❑ Informing clients of sales and holding clothes until the sales starts or arranging for retroactive credit.

Some stores have a separate area for to woo customers. Saks has Fifth Avenue Clubs with refreshments and bathrobes.

Barneys	Special dressing rooms and free beverages in NY and Beverly Hills.
Bergdorf	You can fax in your request.
Bloomingdale's	All stores offer personal shoppers.
Neiman Marcus	Number of personal shoppers varies.
Nordstrom	All stores offer personal shoppers
Saks Fifth Avenue Club	*Fortune Magazine* reported Saks had the most posh of all the clubs.

Having personal shoppers is a service strategy. Since all department stores carry everything you need, why would you choose Macy's over Bloomingdale's? If you had someone who was on your side, getting you that eighteen-inch collar shirt, finding the matching tie or scarf, you will return to that **person**.

Note: Employee retention is important. Companies have tried to lure away service personnel, real estate agents, financial advisors, and others because **it is the person that**

is trusted, not the company. Sometimes the employees leave, as American Express can testify, to set up a competitive venture.

Bridal Registry

Target, a discounter, and even Menards, a home supply chain, offer this service.

Other Registries

Examples include:
- ❑ Federated Department Stores (Macy's, Rich's, Burdine's) started a **Gift Registry** in November 1996.
- ❑ Target stores started a **Lullaby Club** in November 1995.
- ❑ Bed Bath and Beyond changed the name of Bridal and Gift Registry to **Gift Registry** in 1997.

Don't Forget Seniors Day

Ames, a discount store, has 10 percent off Tuesdays. Everything, even goods already on sale, is an additional 10 percent off. One Wal-Mart offers a free McDonald's breakfast and a mini-bingo where the prizes are special discounts on items.

One Target store in 1973 had a Seniors Day in December from 8 a.m. to 10 a.m., just before the December holidays. Now all the stores have a special day where seniors get 10 percent off. Free gift wrapping is the icing on the cake, and the local high school, for a donation to the choir, provides carolers.

Best Practice

Make the registry easy to find.
This is Lowe's on-line Gift Registry logo.

Retail Loyalty: Number of Stores

Loyalty is often said to be a function of availability. Not so. Availability is related to revenue, so the more stores you have, the more you could sell. Both Talbot and Lord & Taylor offered hip clothes instead of professional business attire, saw revenue drop, and their clientele of professional women find alternatives. More stores would just have caused more pain. Both realized that **having repeat customers** means **providing what the customers want**.

How important is having repeat customers? K-Mart estimated that if their best customers increased their visits from 3.4 to 4.0, it would add 2.8 billion to the top line.[28]

Retail: Private Label Clothing

Private labels in department stores offer several advantages:
- ❏ They offer higher profit to the store.
- ❏ They can become a brand.
- ❏ They can be extended to non-clothing.

Arizona, by J.C. Penney, started as jeans and has now been extended into clothing and backpacks.

Store	Jean Brand	Brand Awareness	Method Used To Create Awareness
Gap	Levis	94%	TV and print ads
K-Mart	Route 66	54%	Ads on MTV
J.C.Penney	Arizona	71%	Ads in Sunday flyers
VF Corp.	Wrangler	91%	TV ads
Sears Roebuck	Canyon River Blues	na	Ad in Sunday flyers
Wal-Mart	Faded Glory	50%	In-store poster

Sales reps

There are several questions a sales manager needs to ask and understand the answers.

Why are the customers buying from you?

What is your share of the customer? (If a customer has five printers and two are ours, we have a 40 percent share.)

What is the degree of customer satisfaction?

Do the sales reps anticipate future customer needs?

What is the sales rep retention rate for customers? Is a customer a customer for life?

Optimal Performance

What is a sales representative's optimal performance? How can you estimate the total potential market revenue a sale rep could capture? To do this calculation you need the following data:

- ❑ the number of closings a sales rep had
- ❑ the win-loss percentage
- ❑ the company's market share and the average revenue per deal.

Number of deals closed (say 50) last year divided by the win-loss percentage (say 20 percent) equals the number of deals the sales rep potentially had (50 / 20% = 250).

250 / the company market share (say 10 percent) equals the total number of deals potentially available (250 / 0.1 = 2,500).

The average revenue per opportunity times the number of opportunities equals the total market revenue.

Sell to Every Segment   Profit Strategy

Most customers can be divided into segments, typically according to price. When a segment is ignored, you are essentially surrendering it to a competitor. Xerox did this with the low-end copier market in the eighties. Detroit did this with small cars. Often these are no-profit zones to the company. **The solution is to create another company so that you can compete in that niche.**

This is what US Air did when it created its low cost, no frill airline.

Hallmark, the "When you care enough to send the very best," card manufacturer and retailer began to offer a line of ninety-nine-cent cards. Nationwide advertising began July 1999. The new line was to compete with American Greetings.

Levis has the "red tab" original and those other tabs, representing lesser-priced jeans, for the discount stores.

Typically **as the price point goes up so does the degree of service, the value provided, or the number of product attributes**. Car manufacturers have three categories of models: standard, deluxe, and luxury. Both Schwab and the banks provide service based upon a customer's value.

Schwab

Schwab has a **tiered approach** to servicing customers. Customer service *teams* that make "warm calls" provide various levels of service depending upon the level of assets they carry:

- ❏ Priority Gold—for those with $1 million in assets
- ❏ Priority Service—for those with $500,000 in assets
- ❏ Schwab 500 Active Trader Service—for those who make at least four trades a month and maintain $50,000 in their account
- ❏ Schwab Select—for those with two monthly trades and $25,000

The top three accounts have access to special Web pages. There is also AdvisorSource, a network of 425 independent money managers. Schwab sees that each independent advisor gets at least one referral a month.

The customer service representatives, formerly order-takers, now provide advice and are encouraged to develop expertise in an area, such as variable annuities, or mutual fund selection.

Service

General Electric announced in 1996 that it was going into services to increase its piece of the pie.[29] They make jet engines; why not service them? A ten-year agreement with British Airways signed March 1996 was for $2.3 billion. They will also service rivals such as Pratt & Whitney for British Air.

They make medical imaging equipment; why not service it? Since 1994 they have had a strategy of servicing all a hospital's medical imaging equipment. They do this by buying up independent service shops and signing exclusive multiyear contracts.

And what is the GE secret?

They do it cheaper than the customer can and pass those savings on to the customer. The customer sees it as a winning proposition. Plus, if you sign a big enough contract, GE follows the Fortune 50 practice of giving free advice to customers in areas such as strategic planning and quality.

Service Strategies

These have worked for many companies in the past. Pick the ones that fit your situation.

Sell your service. (Some companies have a paradigm that it is free or non-existent.)

Put your people at their site.

Combine product sales with service agreements.

Partner with companies (they manufacture, you provide the service). Siebel sells software and brokers out the training because they only want to do the software.

Be the vendor that companies **outsource to.**

Be aware of who is moving into town and buying new equipment or building a new plant that they want up and running at minimal cost.

Get into one division (of Honeywell, GM, Dow) and then spread out.

Get service and repair personnel to provide input to new products or their variants so that they are easier to service. Track warranty repairs and parts impacted so that the problem does not continue into the next release.

Have the same codes for service across products.

Sign product **service agreements for three to four years** to provide some stability.

Capture a growth company and grow with them. (e.g. in Minnesota that would be Medtronic or Lawson; in Seattle that would have been Microsoft. Check out your local high-tech council or business "incubator.")

Consider remanufacture and parts repair services.

Does the concept of a "kit" apply? (The army will change an entire subsystem and then finds the "bad" part back in the shop.)

When the product comes to the end of its useful life, what are your pricing actions? Common practices are to allow a trade-in in exchange for a price discount. After a certain period of time customers are billed for materials and labor rather than by monthly contract.

Beware of customers filing for bankruptcy—get paid within thirty days. Best practice is to have **automatic electronic payments.**

Think Big

There is an advantage to being big, especially if you are not restricted by tight job descriptions.

Big Stores

Customers are more likely to purchase impulse goods as they are maneuvering through the store. Larger store formats typically have more sales per square foot.

Retailers can spread fixed costs like management and cleaning over a larger revenue base. Cashiers can be used to stock shelves when the customer flow is down.

Big Offerings

Hershey's Kisses® chocolates get bigger close to Valentines Day. Toilet paper used to come in single rolls; now it comes in packs of twelve to twenty-four rolls.

The Cirque du Soleil has front-row tickets for $65, but if you want to eat before the show, you can buy a package for $160.

Six packs of Pepsi are replaced with cartons of twelve or twenty-four cans.

Photo used with permission of
Hershey Foods Corporation.
HERSHEY's Milk Chocolate candy bar.

Think Small

What happens when you have saturated the market with big stores? When revenue will not increase because you cannot find locations—think small!

CompUSA targeted seven small towns in Texas, close enough to monitor the experiment while too small to require a superstore.[30]

Food portions are shrinking, from mini M&Ms to mini Oreo cookies.

Home Depot has four Villager Hardware stores to compete with strip malls and to fit into smaller downtown spaces.

McDonald's has smaller restaurants in Wal-Marts and other discounters with a limited food selection.

Sears franchises small hardware stores.

Simeks Meats, a meat processor, is partnering with a petrol chain to sell its meats in their convenience stores. There are over 2,000 of these stores.

Staples has twenty-one Staples Express stores in downtown locations aimed at office workers. They also are located in airports.

Wal-Mart in 2002 began to develop traditional-sized supermarkets that will use the Wal-Mart purchasing power, but be closer to shoppers. Called "Neighborhood Markets," they are aiming to compete with Kroger, Albertson's, and Safeway, the top three grocery chains in the United States.

Tiered Pricing

Charge Less to Make More

Many industries, such as financial services, move toward tiered pricing as a way to attract and retain their most valuable customers.

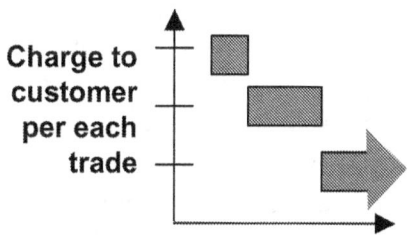

# of trades per quarter

Is someone making seventy-five trades a month worth only $5 a trade, when someone making only two trades a month can be charged $20? Yes. Especially if the financial firm makes a market, meaning it bought the stock and can make a profit on the spread between what the on-line trader will pay and what the firm paid for the stock. Sometimes it is not obvious to charge less to get more.

Provide More Value to Make More

A dealership offers a better deal and sells more cars before the end of the month. The dealership receives an extra 1 percent rebate from the manufacturer.

To motivate sales, provide extra points on certain products. Sales will be motivated to push those products.

Buy more and the retail store gives you free delivery. Office Depot offers free delivery for orders of $50 or more and Amazon.com offers free shipping if the on-line order was greater than $99.

Training

Education: Many Companies' Secret Weapon.

In 1997 Procter & Gamble was facing flat sales for Tampax tampons. Sales in Western Europe, the U.S., and Canada were dropping. In Mexico only 2 percent of women used tampons. To capture this market, education was the answer. Groups of women were invited to a soda party for explanations and free samples. Presentations were held in local shops.

One problem included overcoming certain myths, such as the falsehood that using a tampon will cause a young woman to lose her virginity. The second problem area was to overcome a cultural bias—the religious idea that use of tampons indicated promiscuity.

MicronPC and Gateway offer "free" training with the purchase of their products.

The Avon lady is now often a certified Beauty Advisor. Training consisted of self-study including videos and audiotapes. After passing a test, the soon-to-be advisor takes two days of training where she or he will do a makeover on a fellow advisor.

Boston Chicken ensures employees know their job. The training is on videotape.

Mager

To guarantee the success of training there is only one best development option: Criterion-Referenced Instruction ® and Instructional Module Design® by Robert Mager from The Center for Effective Performance. (770-458-4080 or 1-800-558-4CEP)

It is the benchmark by which others are measured. Whether it be task analysis, skills hierarchies, or determining if there is even a need for training, these courses are the foundation for good instructional designs that involve tasks and behaviors. (www.cepworldwide.com)

New training managers and HR managers responsible for training who do not have a Masters in Instructional Design should consider the Training Managers Workshop.

Due to the rapid change in authorware for CD-ROMS, there is no recommendation at this time.

Waste of Time

Beware of classes with three hundred students—they are usually more for entertainment than instruction. While video and distance learning can teach cognitive skills, behaviors and manual skills need practice. Common sense mandates you wouldn't want a heart surgeon who learned only by video. You would want some hands-on experience before he or she started to work on you.

Understanding and Doing are not the same.

(Note, CDs and computer-based training are excellent tools for providing information, drills, and practice exercises.)

Mandated Training

Mandated training should be tied to business results or have significant business impact. Beware of mandated training that does not include skills and demonstrations of the skills.

Change Management

Change Management that involves training needs to include:

- ❑ What specifically has to be done, in the form of the big picture,
- ❑ How to do it, with a process and "how-to" skills,
- ❑ Why we need to do it, in the form of the logic and urgency (this enables empowerment),
- ❑ A champion to make sure the change takes (this is typically a senior manager whose bonus is tied to the success of the change), and
- ❑ Supports are in place to ease transition.

Use the Old in New Ways

Using the old in new ways provides you the advantage of having brand extensions, thus providing the customer with a known entity and reducing your Awareness (advertising) costs.

Imagine Doublemint gum combined with Crest toothpaste; a gum that prevents cavities and cleans your teeth.

Arm and Hammer Baking Powder is now specially boxed for refrigerators. It absorbs odors with a new "flow through container."

Medications that work in humans can also work in pets. We won't mention which ones lest you go to a vet.

Mars does car repair, such as fixing cracked bumpers. The skills are transferable to repairing boats.

Hershey's Kisses are wrapped in silver, except when they are wrapped in red, green, and gold for the holidays and red for Valentines Day. They also have a giant kiss for Valentines Day.

Tennis balls were repackaged as Fetch Em's for dog owners.

United Parcel Service

USP delivers packages. Would you believe they also deliver the mail? Well they do, sort of. The U.S. Postal Service rules grant two-cent discounts on first-class mail to anyone mailing sixty pieces at once. So UPS picks up the mail and turns the sacks over to a third party for delivery to the post office. Regulations also offer discounts if letters or items like annual reports are taken to postal distribution centers. Letters can even be printed out in different cities and then taken to the local post office to receive a discount.

Eli Lilly and Co.

Eli Lilly sells Sarafem, which is actually Prozac. Sarafem is for premenstrual dysphoric disorder, a severe form of premenstrual syndrome. The pink and lavender pill is targeted at women in ads on TV and in women's magazines.

ATMs

"Enhanced" ATMs sell postage stamps, long-distance phone minutes, subway cards, and tickets to sporting events or plays, as well as the more traditional services such as allowing users to deposit money, get mini-statements, send money orders, transfer funds, and get cash.

When Everyone Zigs, You Zag

Zagging when everyone else zigs means to taking a contrary position to what is the norm. It might mean going smaller like Carmike Cinemas or creative marketing as AT&T did with cell phones and McDonald's. Below are several examples.

- ✪ Carmike Cinemas, Inc., concentrates movie theaters in midsized towns with populations *under 100,000.* (1996) Wal-Mart had a similar strategy. The advantage is in keeping below the competition's radar screen until you grow big enough to have similar economies of scale.

- ℂ CellStar is a *wholesale* distributor of cellular telephones. In addition to *retail* stores, it had over one hundred *kiosks* in Sam's Clubs. (1996)

- ☎ AT&T used McDonald's as a channel for cellular phones in 1997. Flyers included a 1-800 number. McDonald's received funding for their Ronald McDonald houses. Do you have a market segment that usually visits McDonald's or Arby's or Taco Bell or the movies or a particular sport or any other venue you could sell through?

- ☛ Dunn Brothers Coffee, a competitor to Starbucks and Caribou, spent $200,000 on stainless steel counters, murals, and a fireplace to open a 1,800 square-foot coffee house in the local Roseville, MN public library. Dunn also pays $40,000 annually in rent. The library, which has a drive-through window for patrons to pick up books, is all smiles. [31]

- 📖 Barnes and Noble Bookstores have coffee shops to keep customers in the store longer. Usually located in malls, they have begun to expand into college campuses. Often universities have graduate extension campuses with no bookstore, but they have one or two student lounges. Barnes and Noble has filled the niche.

- ✈ UPS has a fleet of airplanes that are not so busy on the weekends. In September 1996, they announced their plans to carry passengers using replaceable seats on their 727 cargo jets.[32] Five aircraft cost about $10 million to retrofit. Conversion can be completed in 3.5 hours for under $1,000. Seating 113, the planes are offered to tour operators for destinations like Aruba and San Juan. They provide three inches more space for passengers, four flight attendants instead of three, and good food.

Appendix B:
Adoption Curve

The most common model to describe aggregate buying behavior is the adoption curve. It essentially says that clients buy in part due to their aversion to risk.

Risk takers, called Innovators, buy new and innovative services and products. Laggards resist purchasing new technologies.

Adoption Curve

At one extreme of the Adoption Curve we have Innovators; they are the first. At the other end we have Laggards. Sometimes this attitude is due to an aversion to technology. Sometimes it is due to disposable income constraints.

Companies can also have revenue constraints, preferring to lease rather than buy.
To use a technology example, Early Adopters had a PDA, or Personal Digital Assistant, five years before the laggards had given up their Rolodex.

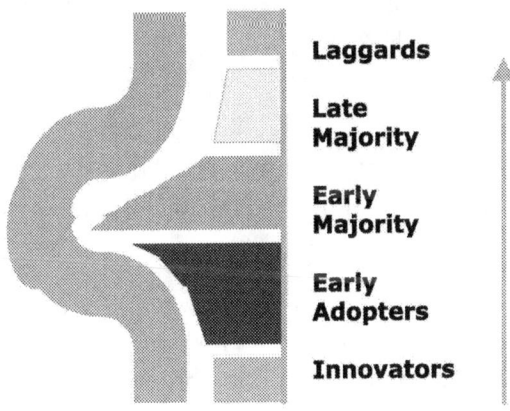

Technology Adoption Curve

This curve refers to the speed at which people and thus companies engage in adopting new technologies.

Innovators

They take pleasure in new technology and, while small in size, the fact that this group bought the offering is an endorsement of the product. They are intrigued by technology. Often they are in a technology field.

Early Adopters

They buy into an offering early. They find it easy to understand the benefits of a technology. They rely on intuition and their own vision of the future.

Early Majority

They are driven by a sense of practicality. They value references and will look at the possibility of winning customers by using technology. They are confident of installing the technology if they choose to purchase it.

Late Majority

They seek to buy from well-established companies. They like to buy something that is standard. They like support, not having the confidence of the Early Majority.

Laggards

To be direct, they do not want the new technology, which by now could be several years old. If the technology is invisible, say hidden in a microprocessor, they will buy it.

How can we describe these persons from a sales perspective?[33]

	Sales Potential	Example: Use of IP Telephony
Laggards	Do not waste time trying to sell to them.	Was upset when a new fax machine was brought into the office. Although it has fax, scanner, and printer capability, it is only used as a fax machine. Does not know or care to know about IP Telephony.
Late Majority	Have proofs when you want to sell to them.	IP Telephony is not on radar screen; looking at cell phones.
Early Majority	One success story will convince them.	Looking at IP options
Early Adopters	Will be Beta Test Sites.	Started IP Telephony in 2000.
Innovators	Read *Fast Company* and are "techies."	Called mother from a PC in 1998. Thought is was cool not having to pay long distance.

Gateways Pricing Challenge Fall 2001

Gateway's 2001 Low Price Guarantee

Dell Computer dropped prices in May 2001. In June 2001, Gateway Computer said they would match any competitor's national ad. It was a limited time promotion to boost their slowing sales, and a response to Dell's aggressive entry into the consumer PC business. It was generally believed that in any price war with Dell, everyone else would lose because Dell had a lower cost of doing business.

So wasn't Gateway's approach flawed? No.

First, it wasn't a war. It was a matching of the nationally advertised price. Yes, it would hurt profits. But people who wanted the Dell price and the warmth of a human could now go to a Gateway Store and kick the tires. (Click the mouse just doesn't sound right.)

Gateway was focusing on consumers. When dealing with consumers the human touch should not be discounted. Schwab discovered this by accident when a relative opened a storefront and sales increased. The low price shoppers, those who would have gone to the Web or the big box retailers, could now consider Gateway. Compaq Computer responded to Dell with ads that stressed style ("our model 5000T comes in four colors") and convenience ("one button on our keyboard takes you to the Internet"). Compaq offered $100 rebates. Gateway also came out with a $999 laptop that had more features.

Second, Gateway had other sources of revenue. For one, they provide training. Best Buy and Circuit City do not offer training. Gateway stores have a room for training. That is an advantage in the consumer market.

Third, Gateway's computer prices in early 2001 often included training. Now training was unbundled and became an additional, chargeable feature. Also, if you go to a store for training, what is the possibility you will buy additional hardware, like more RAM or a scanner down the road?

Gateway is matching commodity to commodity: RAM to RAM; gigs of hard drive to gigs of hard drive.

What Gateway lacked is a Wow feature. When you have a Wow or Sizzle feature you can charge a premium. Gateway does offer value-added packages for music or video enthusiasts. Chances are that they will be able to upsell their customers.

When you provide value-added services from the Customer Use Cycle you can either charge for it or make it part of a bundled package.

You can also delete it. Gateway bundled training with its PC prices earlier in the year, however the training became extra as prices dropped.

(As the first edition of this book went to press, Gateway announced a massive layoff of 25 percent. They are also closing about 10 percent of their stores—the ones with the least amount of traffic. Their ads do not speak to matching Dells prices. Their August 2001 ads used a metaphor showing an employee holding a *grocery bag* full of french fries implying that you **get more with Gateway**. By December 2001 the ads showed a cow talking to the CEO and discussing **value-added** packages such as digital photography. Dell Computer ended 2001 promoting its $899 computer on the SciFi channel and other places parents and back-to-school college students might see the promotion. Gateway countered by promoting a $799 PC.) On January 8, 2002, IBM announced it was outsourcing the manufacture of its PC hardware.

Endnotes

1 Youngblood, Dick. "Simek's gets ready to beef up," *Star Tribune* (Minnesota), 14 November 1999. p. D3.

2 Shirouzu, Norihiko. "P&G's Joy makes an Unlikely Splash in Japan" *WSJ*, 10 December 1997 p. B1.

3 Leiber, Ronald B. "Hey, it's a tough business," *Fortune*, 17 February 1997, p. 140.

4 Susan Lowe reported that the legal industry did the best in terms of knowing how promotions brought in the new clients, while the information technology industry was well below average. (978-287-5080, slowe@expertisemarketing.com)

5 Howard, Theresa. "AFLAC cuck gives wings to insurer's name recognition," *USA Today*, 17 May 2001, p. 9B.

6 McLean, Bethany. "Duck and Coverage," *Fortune*, 13 August 2001, p. 142

7 In 2002 Dr. Pepper ran TV ads featuring country western singer Garth Brooks.

8 Jacobs, April. "Intel pulling back from selling NetStructure brand," *Network World*, 20 November 2000, p. 10.

9 Reported Patricia Cicala, analyst at the Gardner Group, 23 November 1998, *Computer World*, p. 54.

10 To save money, many retailers take advantage of low-cost municipal loans. Wegmans, a supermarket chain headquartered in upstate New York, often uses low-interest state loans to build new stores. The downtown Pittsburgh Lazarus store was built with city development funds. Payments back to the city were tied to revenue. In the fiscal year that ended January 31, 2000, the store's revenue was only $20.6 million. If it had been the $41.7 million hoped for by city officials, Lazarus would have had to pay a $13 million construction loan. Lord & Taylor received a subsidy of $11.7 million to build its store in a converted bank in downtown Pittsburgh.

11 Serwer, Andy. "The last hot computer stock," *Fortune* (magazine, US edition). 11 May 1998

[12] Nations Business, September 1998, A total solution to improve sales by Michael Galvin, p.6

[13] Pertersen, Melody. "Some Drug Companies Use Price Increases to Spur Wholesale Buying and Lift Sales in the Short Run." *The New York Times*. March 5, 2002. Page C8

[14] Russell, Joy D. "IBM's Big Partner Agenda." VARBusiness 17 January, 2002 page 19

[15] Lee, Thomas. "Creating Demand for a New Product." *Nations Business, August 1998, p. 11*

[16] Carter, Bill. "CBS is divided of the use of false images in broadcasts." *New York Times,* 13 Jan 2000, p. C1.

[17] Soloman, Jay. "Back From Brink, Korea Inc. Wants A Little Respect." *The Wall Street Journal*. 13 June 2002. Page A1.

[18] Yeoman's Michael. "Recycled Retailers." *The Pittsburgh Tribune-Review*. 10 July 2002. Page B8.

[19] Leung, Shirley. "At McDonalds's will 'Extension' Join the Menu?" *The Wall Street Journal*. 29 May 2002 Page B1

[20] Ibid.

[21] Green, Richard. "Toro Charges Into Greener Fields with New Products." *The Wall Street Journal.*. July 22, 1997, page B4,.

[22] Feder, Barnaby. "Flip that burger faster." *Star Tribune* (MN), July 24,1997, page E3. Reprint from *The New York Times*.

[23] Smith, Geoffrey and Keenan, Faith. "Kodak is the picture of digital success." *Business Week*. 14 January 2002 page 39.

[24] Angwin, Julia. "Service—With a Side of Sales." *The Wall Street Journal*. 29 October 2001. p. R13.

[25] Carton, Barbara. "PCs Replace Lettuce Tubs at Sales Parties." *The Wall Street Journal*. March 26,1997, page B1.

[26] Wilson Craig, "Celebration sells a family lifestyle." *USA Today,* July 3, 1997, page D1.

[27] Carver, Jim. "Your Super Utility." *The Denver Post*. 17 August, 1997, Page 1J

[28] *Business Week*, 9 April 2001 Page 51

[29] Jack Welch's encore. *Business Week*. October 28,1996, page 155-9

[30] Henderson, Angelo. "Death watch?" *The Wall Street Journal.* 18 July 1997. Page A1.

[31] Bentley, Rosalind. "Public Library as Intellectual mall." *Star Tribune* (MN), p. E1

[32] Blackman, Douglas. "UPS, Feeling Boxed In, Stages its Own Growth." *The Wall Street Journal.* September 17, 1996, page B4. *The Sunday NY Times,* 4/27/97 had an extended article on UPS. In 2001 UPS suspended service. The business was profitable, however they decided to focus on their core business.

[33] Rogers, E. M. (1995). *Diffusion of innovations,* Fourth edition. New York: The Free Press

Index

For additional information
On courses and coaching or workshops, contact:
KobiJames@BusinessMentors.com

0-595-24410-6

www.ingramcontent.com/pod-product-compliance
Lightning Source LLC
Chambersburg PA
CBHW080009210526
45170CB00015B/1958